MULTI-SCREEN MARKETING

MULTI-SCREEN MARKETING

The Seven Things You Need to Know to Reach Your Customers across TVs, Computers, Tablets, and Mobile Phones

NATASHA HRITZUK
KELLY JONES

WILEY

Cover design and illustration: George Neill

Published by John Wiley & Sons, Inc., Hoboken, New Jersey.
Published simultaneously in Canada.

For general information about our other products and services, please contact our Customer
Care Department within the United States at (800) 762-2974, outside the United States at
(317) 572-3993 or fax (317) 572-4002.

Wiley publishes in a variety of print and electronic formats and by print-on-demand. Some
material included with standard print versions of this book may not be included in e-books or
in print-on-demand. If this book refers to media such as a CD or DVD that is not included in
the version you purchased, you may download this material at http://booksupport.wiley.com.
For more information about Wiley products, visit www.wiley.com.

Library of Congress Cataloging-in-Publication Data:

Hritzuk, Natasha.
    The multi-screen marketing : the seven things you need to know to reach your customers
    across TVs, computers, tablets, and mobile phones / Natasha Hritzuk, Kelly Jones.
      pages cm
    Includes index.
    ISBN 978-1-118-89902-1 (cloth); ISBN 978-1-118-90076-5 (ebk);
    ISBN 978-1-118-90080-2 (ebk)
      1. Internet marketing.   2. Electronic commerce.   I. Jones, Kelly.   II. Title.
  HF5415.1265.H75   2014
  658.8'72—dc23

                                                      2013051131

Printed in the United States of America
10 9 8 7 6 5 4 3 2 1

CONTENTS

ACKNOWLEDGMENTS

Thank you to our talented Consumer Insights team—Anita Caras, Esther Burke, Ivy Esquero, James Comer, Jian Yang, Jocelyn Richie, Linda Liberg, Martyn Crook, Natasha Moisio, and Phil Jones—who, with passion, skill, and an innovative mindset, are committed to bringing a human face to data and technology; Shelley Zalis, Maury Giles, Whitney Cornell, Caroline Van Sickle, Boris Musa, Wendy Weng, Steve MacBeth, Steven Webster, Chloe Fowler, Richard Fraser, Christian Claussen, and Alexei Orlov for their brilliant insights and case studies; George Neill, our resident Renaissance Man and cover designer, for demonstrating that he is truly our Maestro of Design; Cabrelle Abel for her remarkable intelligence and patience; our Microsoft marketing and PR teams for their amazing support of Thought Leadership and Consumer Insights; our sales team, who embraced our work and provided the opportunities for us to test and share our ideas with customers; the teams at Ipsos OTX, Flamingo, Razor Research, The Modellers, and The Future Laboratories for their considerable contributions to our research over the years; to Richard Narramore, Tiffany Colón, Lauren Freestone, and the Wiley team; and finally, to Rick Chavez for his advocacy of Consumer Insights, for being a great sounding board and a consummate ideas man . . . and for somehow not firing us at any point in this process.

On a personal note, from Natasha: thank you to my family, Grant and Rosalind, who patiently endure my travel schedule, odd work hours, and permanently open computer. You make coming home every day the best reward anyone could hope for;

my parents, Lois, John, and Jim ("Cricket") for their support, encouragement, and love; and to my friends who bring levity, great conversation, and joy into my life.

From Kelly: thank you to Korry, Marly, and Erin, true soul sisters each; Ron and Nancy Jones for their never-ending support; and to Rob for all of the reasons, all of the time.

The Seven Things You Need to Know to Reach Your Customers across Televisions, Computers, Tablets, and Mobile Phones

It's Monday morning, and an average American consumer—let's call her Stacy—wakes up to her alarm on her mobile phone. She checks her calendar in bed, then showers after turning on her favorite morning televsion program. While she jams a piece of bread in the toaster and wakes up her kids, she checks her mobile weather app and replies to a few e-mails. Then, while her husband gets the kids ready for school, she's off and running—out of the house and into her car.

On her commute, she takes a conference call on her mobile phone and uses an app to find which gas station has the cheapest gas near her office. At work, she alternates between her mobile and laptop, often taking a few minutes to browse her favorite shopping sites and check her children's school website. She runs by the grocery store in the evening, using a coupon on her phone when she checks out at the register. Once home, she grabs a recipe from her tablet, watches a video her friend sent her, and plays a quick game on her Xbox with her kids before dinner. After they go to bed, she relaxes with her tablet in front of the television with her husband and gets a little work done on her laptop. In short, she's online, she's mobile, and she's moving between multiple screens. And that's just Monday.

Now, let's look at a typical marketer. We'll call her Jen. Jen runs a small clothing boutique focusing on casual work attire for professional women. She knows her customer is busy. And she knows that her customer, like Stacy, is consuming content across televisions, computers, tablets, and mobile phones every day. But she doesn't know how to capture her customers' attention. Her local televsion spot is expensive and nearly impossible to measure. Her search campaign takes hours to manage. She hates printing up postcards and buying up direct mail lists when she knows her postcards are tossed out with the day's recycling. She's constantly barraged by businesses that say they can help, but they typically specialize in one trendy thing—mobile apps or social campaigns—without linking to the big picture. Jen doesn't want more Facebook "likes," she wants to improve her bottom line.

Sound familiar? Now, more than ever before, your customers' time is precious, and their attention is divided. At its simplest, being where your customer is spending her time is why multi-screen advertising is vital for brands to stay relevant, effective, and competitive. So why aren't all campaigns multi-screen by default?

Multi-screen marketing in its current form is not exactly simple. As marketers, we've grown used to running traditional campaigns across new forms of digital media. Yet we're still using traditional methods of buying, executing, and measuring campaigns, partly because it's hard to keep up with new technologies and the ways consumers are using them. But we're often taking chances where we shouldn't and nearly always not getting enough bang for our marketing buck. Big branding campaigns tend to gravitate toward the richness and large audiences of television, whereas direct response campaigns have favored the immediacy and measurability of channels like search. Programmatic buying—the practice of purchasing audiences via real-time bidding, retargeting, and behavioral targeting—has become increasingly attractive due to its scale and efficiency, and video across all channels has become an essential extension of our brand campaigns. Meanwhile, mobile, social, and local agencies have popped up seemingly overnight, insisting on line items for each new channel. Marketing budgets have splintered to address these seemingly divergent media silos, with different agencies handling different types of campaign or media buys.

In short, today's marketing strategies are structured by devices and the traditional marketing ecosystems swarming around them. But is it all really working? We believe there's an easier way to market to your customers across screens. And here's the good news: you don't need to be a big-budgeted Fortune 500 company with seven agencies on speed dial to accomplish it.

We travel all over the world speaking to brand marketers and their agencies about how to use consumer insights to drive smarter multi-screen marketing strategies. And it doesn't matter if they have marketing teams of 1 or 1,001; all marketers struggle with the same challenges when it comes to reaching and engaging consumers across screens. In a world where device and media proliferation is the new reality, marketers like Jen face an overwhelming array of new uncertainties. *Is it sufficient to advertise on television only? When should mobile factor into the media mix? Do I need to craft unique creative messages for different devices, such as tablets? How should I be preparing for newer form factors, such as augmented reality and mobile payment? How does it all work together? And most important, how do I know any of this new media is even working?*

Ironically, the very same technological breakthroughs that are supposed to be positioned to help businesses only amplify the complexity of reaching consumers with the right message at the right time. With separate social and mobile line-items appearing in nearly every advertising request for proposal (RFP), marketers often rely on a technology-first approach, where they focus on the capabilities of the device, rather than the needs of the consumer. This approach obscures the fact that these devices are just physical objects without any intrinsic meaning when divorced from the people who use them. Most marketers aren't aware that they are using a device or technology-first approach. It's simply been the way we have done things since the dawn of the television era. But in a multi-screen world, this approach takes too many resources and results in wasted budgets.

While it may be surprising to hear a pair of consumer-insights researchers who work for a technology company say that our industry's current obsession with device-centric strategies is wrongheaded, that's exactly what we're going do.

In 2010, when I joined Microsoft from General Mills, I knew I was making a big professional leap from the consumer packaged goods (CPG) sector into technology. In the world of CPG, the consumer is at the heart of everything you do—from product development to branding and communications. It has to be. Without in-depth consumer insights, commoditized products like cereal or bottled water would lack any meaningful differentiation. In the world of technology, however, software and devices are at the heart of most strategies, and the expectation is often a form of magical thinking depicted in the movie *Field of Dreams*: if you build it, they will come. Given this chasm, I assured myself that at least I was in the digital media business, which would function as a bridge between these two worlds: deploying devices and technology to connect brands and products to consumers. After a few months into the job, however, I realized this bridge was more illusory than real. It became pretty clear to me that the digital media playbook was grounded in the "build it and they will come" paradigm, and consumers were cast in a surprisingly recessive role.

Consider a mom away from her family on a business trip—let's call her Sarah. Sarah uses Skype every night to catch up with her family, read her child a bedtime story virtually, and be "home" just as she would if she weren't away. Skype is not just a video chatting product or piece of technology untethered from a human being; it's an enabler of a very specific need. For Sarah, it's an enabler of her need to be a good mother, even when she's away. Technology, therefore, is only as good as the human needs it serves. People, with all their nuances, contradictions, and complexities, are still at the helm. And yet many marketers would see this interaction as only a series of data points: a consumer's gender, the amount of time she spends on a video chatting service, and perhaps the time of day she does it. And as a result, they might inundate her with ads that are completely irrelevant to her needs at that moment. She might get ads for shopping deals based on her current location, but she's not interested in shopping in Omaha while on her business trip; she wants to connect with her family back home. So simply relying on location or demographics is not a successful way to reach Sarah.

So how did consumers get lost in the digital shuffle? Why are marketing campaigns organized around devices instead of around customer needs? Unintentionally and incrementally. In other words, no one has deliberately set out to marginalize consumers, and there has been no single watershed moment when consumers were decisively pushed into the background. We believe there are three major factors that have landed us here: first, the functional complexity of digital devices; second, the way media is bought and sold; and third, the legacy of a television-dominated advertising world. The combination of these factors has driven consumers into the background and ultimately complicated our ability to market to them effectively in a multi-screen world.

FUNCTIONS AND FEATURES: WHERE ARE CONSUMERS IN THE MIX?

If you think about traditional media, there isn't a tremendous amount of complexity in terms of what consumers actually *do* with each media channel: they look at magazines and read newspapers; they listen to the radio; and they watch programs on television. As a result, figuring out how to land advertising on these media is reasonably straightforward: visual for magazines and newspapers, auditory for radio, and a combination of both for television.

When one factors in digital media, however, things get a bit more complicated. Each device in the digital space, from the personal computer to the smartphone, is multi-functional by design. A laptop computer with Internet access embodies myriad functions, including word processing, mapping systems, reference libraries, trip planners, social connection capabilities, and entertainment hubs. Mobile devices like smartphones and tablets take the functionality of computers, shrink them down into smaller packages, and layer in a few additional functions, including digital cameras and video. Suddenly, your computer is pocket-sized and completely portable.

But as a digital marketer, how can you possibly begin to think about delivering content on these complex, multi-functional devices? The most intuitive approach is to identify the primary "thing" these devices do—word processing, searching, video streaming, location mapping—and focus on delivering advertising within these functions. And in fact, this is what has happened today. We stick a pre-roll ad within a video and place it on a mobile phone or a big screen games console. Another approach is to focus on the device's technological features. For tablets and smartphones, we know that they're portable, they have touch screens, and they support apps. So we develop local, in-app campaigns. But the more we focus on functions and features, the further away we get from the people who are using these devices; the further we get from the people using these devices, the greater the risk that we build marketing campaigns that are technologically clever, but fail to build bridges between consumers and brands.

Arguably, we haven't even mastered the art of digital advertising on single devices, yet now we're confronted with the even bigger challenge of how to create campaigns that flow across multiple screens. Marketers typically default to simply taking their strategy for advertising on a single screen and applying it everywhere. But the technological feature approach falls flat when applied to more than two screens; mobile phones and tablets are portable, but televisions and computers aren't. So creating a campaign based on mobility isn't multi-screen advertising—it's single-screen advertising applied to multiple screens. Similarly, touch screens and apps are predominantly mobile- and tablet-feature dependent, so campaigns that capitalize on these capabilities don't play to the strengths of less portable screens.

On the surface finding a common "thing" that each screen does, seems like the most straightforward way to tackle multi-screen complexity. *People watch content on televisions, computers, mobile phones, and tablets, so let's take our television campaign and just push it across each screen. Simple!* But this approach assumes that consumers relate to each screen in the same way because the screens do similar things. As we'll discuss in Chapter 2, consumers have very distinct relationships with each screen, which means advertising content needs to be adapted accordingly. Without understanding these nuances, marketers risk taking great content that works on one screen and incrementally reducing its effectiveness as they apply it across each additional screen.

To create truly effective multi-screen marketing, we need to bring our focus away from device functions and features and turn it back to consumers. Going back to Sarah's example, that means not geotargeting her video experience just because geotargeting is a capability, and instead focus first on Sarah's needs, then on how the functionality of the device can serve them.

LAUNCHING CAMPAIGNS ON MULTIPLE SCREENS IS NOT MULTI-SCREEN MARKETING

A second factor complicating marketers' ability to successfully engage consumers across screens is the way media is sold and purchased. Traditionally, media agencies are structured to sell by device or channel, which, by definition, places the consumer in the background and makes it incredibly challenging to knit together a cohesive multi-screen campaign strategy.

When separate teams develop strategies for traditional and digital media, the overarching outcome is weak integration between television and digital screens. If digital media is further broken down into separate silos for search, mobile, social, and gaming, the fragmentation is even more pronounced. This fragmentation ultimately leads to separate campaigns and strategies for television, display media, programmatic media, mobile, social, and search. The biggest fallacy is that marketing campaigns on multiple screens translate into genuine multi-screen marketing. And yet ironically, running campaigns on a bunch of different screens only leads to marketing complexity and consumer bewilderment. According to a study we conducted in 2010, 80 percent of consumers expect their experiences to be improved through cohesive—not fragmented—multi-screen marketing.[1] Brands that ignore this rising expectation risk driving a wedge between themselves and their customers.

From a marketer's perspective, fragmented multi-screen campaigns make marketing incredibly and needlessly complicated. How do you create content and find the time, money, and resources to build different campaigns that hit all the varying media channels? Are you genuinely and effectively connecting consumers to your brands, products, and services by simultaneously driving social, mobile, television, and search campaigns? How do you begin to understand the aggregate impact and return on investment of these campaigns? It's hard enough to measure the success of mobile and social campaigns, let alone the total impact of all these different campaigns together.

Placing marketing on a lot of different screens presupposes that consumers are using devices in a similarly fragmented way, which we know is absolutely not the case.[2] The entire push to create multi-screen campaigns versus marketing on multiple screens is driven by endless amounts of data that show consumers are absorbing content across screens simultaneously and seamlessly. As is often the case, consumers are operating steps ahead of marketers, and we're struggling to find a way to catch up to them.

It would be pretty bold to sit here as consumer insights professionals and suggest that we solve for fragmentation and disconnected marketing across screens by calling for all media agencies to restructure. *Hey—we have a great idea, drop the silos and just merge all media selling into one group!* If it were simple to effect massive infrastructural change, media agencies would have reorganized years ago. An easier way to reduce some of the complexity and disconnection that results from fragmented media selling and buying is to put the consumer at the center of your multi-screen strategy. If you begin by understanding how consumers use different screens—and even more important, what they are trying to accomplish across these screens—clear patterns emerge. These consumer-driven patterns subsequently guide how marketing campaigns are developed. As we will argue throughout this book, focusing on consumers creates clarity because there is order and predictability in human needs and motivations. And in a complex, multi-screen world, finding these patterns and responding to them doesn't just make marketing easier, it also makes marketing better. We want to move away from marketing on lots of screens to connecting consumers to brands across screens seamlessly, meaningfully, and effectively.

THE LEGACY OF TELEVISION

It is very difficult to create effective multi-screen advertising when we haven't figured out how to evaluate whether these campaigns are delivering against brand and sales goals. As an industry, we're still wrestling with how to measure digital, social, and mobile campaigns in a meaningful way, so it's not surprising that we still haven't determined the best way to measure multi-screen campaigns. This inability to measure whether these campaigns actually work leads to a couple of big problems.

First, marketers are loathe to invest in something if they can't prove it works. Even if a marketing manager *thinks* a multi-screen campaign will be more effective than a standalone television campaign, she isn't going to stake millions of dollars in a multi-screen strategy based on gut instinct. Second, even if the marketing manager works for a company that is comfortable with activating media plans and campaigns that can't be fully measured (a rare thing, indeed), it is incredibly difficult to refine and optimize campaigns if you can't assess what's working and what isn't. And since part of the appeal of online campaigns is the ability to iterate in real time, this scenario is incredibly problematic.

One of the big challenges underlying this measurement conundrum can be tracked to the dominant legacy of television. We've mastered the art of measuring how well television campaigns work with the help of Nielsen ratings and Gross Rating Points (GRPs). Marketers can make well-informed decisions about when and where to advertise on television to achieve their goals, whether it's to increase sales or to draw attention to a brand or new product. Having this level of understanding and being able to make precise decisions around placing media on one screen makes it difficult to enter a world where you are operating in the dark. And so we enter the arena of the chicken and the egg: how will marketers work up the courage to invest in multi-screen campaigns if they can't prove that they're effective? But if too few marketers venture into the terra incognita of multi-screen marketing, we'll struggle to find effective ways to measure whether they work.

Rather than throw up our hands, let's go with what we know. We know how to measure campaign effectiveness on television, so why not take what works for television and apply it to the other screens? This isn't a bad way to start, since it is helpful to have one metric that can be applied across screens; it's certainly a better starting point than having different metrics across different screens. But we're making a lot of assumptions when we decide to apply television metrics to other screens.

Assumption one: All screens deliver content to consumers in a similar way.

Assumption two: All screens drive similar results to television.

Assumption three: Consumers use each screen the same way and for the same reasons.

Assumption four: Existing metrics are meaningful in the digital age.

As you read through each of these four assumptions, it's clear they don't ring true. Using television-based metrics to assess whether media works on other devices is the ultimate case of a device-first strategy. Throughout this book, we'll show that consumers relate to each screen, as well as screens in combination, in unique ways, so the manner in which marketers deliver content across each screen needs to be distinct. This has real implications for how we measure whether a campaign is working (or not) on each screen. Consumers also turn to different screens to achieve basic goals and meet basic needs, as we'll show in our Digital Goal-State research, which means we need to start thinking about whether campaigns are delivering against consumer goals, not just marketer objectives. Shifting focus from devices to consumers starts to shed light on how we can resolve some of these larger cross-screen measurement issues. And critically, consumer-centricity helps to drive clarity around what we want to measure and what success looks like from a marketer *and* a consumer perspective.

In light of the challenges we've laid out so far, we do have some good news: it's not as complicated as you think. In *Multi-Screen Marketing: The Seven Things You Need to Know to Reach Your Consumers across Televisions, Computers, Tablets, and Mobile Phones*, we take a unique consumer-centric approach to understanding why people use devices and digital services in order to bring the consumer firmly back into focus. We explore how consumers relate to each screen differently, illustrating that a "one size fits all screens" content strategy fails to deliver what consumers are actually seeking. We will establish the importance of adjusting content that fits the unique way consumers relate to each device, and then explore what happens when screens come together and are used in increasingly fluid and interchangeable ways. We'll augment our findings with real-world examples from marketers who are embracing a consumer-centric approach to multi-screen marketing, and we'll provide ways companies can use technology in service to people, rather than the other way around. And throughout, we'll invoke our guiding philosophy the "why behind the what."

THE WHY BEHIND THE WHAT

We live in a data-rich world. And data provides a sense of security and certainty—*if a number tells me something, it must be true!* But in the media and marketing worlds, the proliferation of data we collect has presented us with a new and often overwhelming challenge: how do I make sense of the data I'm getting from televsions, computers, tablets, and mobile phones?

Every time someone searches for hotels in Palm Springs, posts a photo of her daughter on Instagram, books a restaurant in Orlando on Open Table, and orders some hand wash from Soap.com, these online journeys and transactions are recorded on servers as single data points. All of these data points become, at their best, a way of providing better services and information to people. But, at their worst, these data points exist as disconnected points of information—single stars in a universe without constellations—that can be nearly impossible to understand or navigate. It's enough to make even the most data-driven marketer yearn for a simpler time when the only data point that counted was how many housewives tuned in to hear their favorite radio soap opera at lunchtime.

In many ways, data has taken on a life of its own. We have immense staffs of people hired to organize it, store it, and mine it for business-critical insights; we hold vast numbers of conferences to share our wins and challenges; and we hire consultants to come in and help us draw maps through the chaos. It's almost as if we believe that the secret to winning in business lies in Big Data; we just need the right data sources and the best talent to uncover the road map to success. But perversely, being overly focused on data can make multi-screen marketing needlessly complex. Here's an example that will help illustrate what we mean.

Baseball has traditionally been a game of statistics. Any real baseball fan will know her ERAs from her RBIs. And as the popular book *Moneyball* proved, there's certainly a way to play the game by the numbers. But consider what happens when you eliminate the context, the "why behind the what" so to speak.

In Game 1 of the 1954 World Series, between the Cleveland Indians and the New York Giants, Willie Mays made a defensive play known far and wide as "The Catch." Mays, arguably one of the greatest players of all time, made thousands of outfield catches during his 22-year career. And while millions of catches have been made in baseball, to date, there has only ever been one catch that is referenced with that capitalized preposition in front of it. *Why?*

The score was 2–2, and it was the top of the eighth inning. Cleveland had runners on first and second. Vic Wertz was up to bat. And with one smooth swing, Wertz crushed a ball to center field. Mays, who was partial to playing shallow so he could make faster throws to the infield, ran backwards to make a spectacular over-the-shoulder catch on the warning track; he immediately pivoted and threw the ball 440 feet to the infield, keeping the slightly shocked Cleveland runner at first from advancing to second. The sheer athleticism of Mays's play went down in history. Wertz was out, and Mays saved the game for the Giants, who eventually swept the World Series. It was a spectacular moment that went well beyond the quantifiable fact of a single outfield catch; it captured the hearts and minds of the fans, and solidified the place of a new national hero.

A great outfield catch, an infield error, a game-winning home run. In and of themselves, all of these can be quantified, counted and measured. That's the way they go down in the record books after all. But those are just the numbers. It's the "why behind the what," the humanizing and often qualitative insight, that stirs the passions of people around the world.

This is not a book about baseball. But the scenario above illustrates the dilemma marketers face: we have data we can look at six ways to Sunday, but all too frequently, we lack real insight—insight that helps us know our customers at a more emotional level—that subsequently enables us to make better and more accurate marketing decisions. It's like the difference between hearing the play-by-play in a Vin Scully baseball broadcast versus trying to recapture the excitement of the game by looking at a penciled-in scorecard.

It has become clear that data has started to obscure the people behind the numbers, in much the same way that our focus on device functions and features has disconnected us from the people behind the screens. We're harboring an illusion that numbers are simple and people are complex. The funny thing is, without a human face to bring meaning, numbers can be misleading, confusing, and often obscure the big picture.

For all of the incredible things data can tell us, it has two shortcomings: it only reveals *what* people do and usually only what they've done in the past. What people do can be unpredictable, changeable, and complicated, and what they did yesterday may or may not help us understand what they'll do tomorrow. We can try to overcome some of these data limitations by building statistical models that help light up what may happen in the future based on what people did in the past. But we need to ensure that these models don't take us further from the people whose actions generated the data to begin with. The more we rely on data exclusively, the more we risk making decisions based on partial insight and that are far removed from those big moments of insight we seek.

In the marketing and media world, we are particularly in love with data. Most of the decisions we make about where, when, and how to connect people to our brands and services are based on data; it gives us a starting point, and it helps us understand whether or not our advertising is working. We gather information from set-top boxes, from cookies, and across mobile phones, tablets, computers, and throughout the digital ecosystem. But our overreliance on data has also started to limit our progress as an industry. Data only tells us half the story. And, in the age of multiple screens and devices, knowing half the story is only serving to distract and confuse us at a time when we need more clarity.

Imagine that you have been asked to create a multi-screen marketing campaign to connect consumers to your brand—in this case, a global hotel chain. You access your vast stores of data and see that your target audience tends to watch television in the mornings and evenings. In the mornings, they're also using their mobile phones and computers. In the evenings, they are active on their tablets, which they use with the television in the background. So you need a campaign that runs on television in the mornings and evenings, but also on mobile phones and computers in the morning and tablets in the evening. Even if you can figure out how to simultaneously run an effective campaign on these different screens, you also need to sort out what channels you will leverage: Search? Social? Video? All of the above?

You dig a bit deeper and gather more data. It appears that over the past few weeks, people have been watching the news in the morning, dramas in the evening, and searching for things like "flights" and "beaches" on their mobile devices, while e-mailing on their computers and tablets. Now you have a bit more information and can make an educated guess about what people are actually doing across these screens: being entertained, doing a bit of research for a beach trip and multi-tasking by catching up on e-mails with colleagues or friends. Based on what you've learned from this data deep dive, it's clear you need to come up with a multi-screen campaign that links a hotel offer at a beach resort with a flight deal. Multi-screen campaign sorted!

But not so fast. You've made a lot of assumptions based on these people's behavior. What if you've made the wrong assumptions? As it turns out, your hotel prospects have not been researching beach trips. Instead, they are deeply concerned by a news story that's been running for a few weeks about an impending hurricane sweeping the Caribbean. Their online searches for flights and beaches are actually motivated by an attempt to figure out if the beaches where they're vacationing are in the path of the storm; they are checking cancellation policies on airline websites, e-mailing their friends to get suggestions on alternate vacation spots, and checking online for flights to destinations not in the eye of the storm. An extreme example, maybe, but by observing what people are doing and not peeling back the layers to understand why, you are missing at least half the picture. So instead of tempting people to book rooms at your beach resorts scattered around the Caribbean, you've just spent a bunch of money on people who have, en masse, decided to cancel their trips to the beach and either stay home or fly elsewhere.

One of our big epiphanies over the past three years is that to market successfully in the multi-screen era, you must understand the "why behind the what." Like our Willie Mays example, a catch isn't always just a catch; there's more to the story. One of the big limitations of being a primarily data- and device-driven industry is that it's impossible to understand why people are doing things if you are making decisions based only on server-data. To get at "the why," you need to refocus your attention on the people behind the numbers. How? By talking to your customers, asking questions, and making an effort to understand their goals, needs, motivations, and values—all of which inform their behaviors. If you think about it, everything we do—sleep, eat, watch reality television, buy $200 jeans, search for beach holidays, post an update on Facebook—is driven by a need, goal, or motivation. The need, goal, or motivation may be trite, trivial, or not very "worthy"—*I buy Rag & Bone jeans because I work hard and have earned the right!*—but that doesn't negate the fact that a need is underpinning the behavior.

Human behavior can be complex, changeable, and unpredictable—but our motivations are typically consistent. One morning you may observe me turning on my television and watching something simultaneously on my tablet. The next morning, I may be watching something on my tablet, but also appear active on my mobile phone. How can we market to people when they are doing things on lots of screens and in ways that aren't always consistent? The answer lies in moving beyond observing *what* I'm doing on my tablet and mobile to actually understanding *why* I'm moving between screens. The "why" may be that this activity is motivated by a need to save for my daughter's college education. I'm watching CNBC, checking stock movements on my tablet, and going to a banking app on my mobile that helps me move money between accounts. Suddenly, the marketing challenge is less daunting. Any brand that helps me fulfill my goal of making the right financial decisions to save for a college education becomes a hero brand for me. So putting a banner ad for a bank that lands simultaneously on my mobile and tablet is not going to cut it. Yes, I may be in a financial services head space, but what I really want is for the bank to give me personalized information, assistance, and options that help me land on the best investment decisions for me.

Multi-screen marketing is not about having a presence on lots of screens. It's about understanding why people are on these different screens, then giving them content that helps them achieve what they've set out to do, whether that's having fun, making a purchase decision, connecting with others, or gathering information. And what we've found time and again is that once you dig beneath what people do and figure out *why*, very clear, consistent, and predictable patterns emerge. These patterns can help unlock the challenges around multi-screen marketing and provide clear road maps for building compelling, meaningful, and memorable campaigns.

At Microsoft, we have many platforms and devices where brands can land their advertising. Our portfolio is, by nature, multi-screen: Xbox, the Surface Tablet, the Lumia Mobile phone, Skype, Bing, and MSN; Windows 8 software drives a consistent visual interface and enables campaigns to flow across these different surfaces and screens. Our challenge in the advertising business is to provide frameworks that help our customers build marketing campaigns that connect consumers to their brands and services across these different platforms. The subsequent frameworks that we've developed through consumer insights research are all focused on driving a consumer-centric orientation so we can understand people's motivations, needs, and goals. These frameworks are increasingly helping our customers and internal teams identify white space opportunities to build multi-screen experiences that are anchored firmly in consumer needs.

To be clear, we are not claiming that our research should replace all of the data we currently use to make marketing and media decisions. We are not making a case that data should be pushed into the background and that numbers should be ignored because they're misleading. Above and beyond alienating a lot of people we respect and like, this sort of extreme view would probably land us in the media equivalent of a loony bin. What we are saying, however, is that we must not forget about the people behind the data and the screens. And we need to dig deeper and go beyond our current preoccupation with *what* people do. What we are advocating, ultimately, is that marketers need to work with a complete picture, a clear understanding of the "why" and the "what." Bringing consumers back to the foreground and making an effort to understand who they are, what they seek, and why they are seeking it is critical to successful marketing in the multi-screen age. If we don't lead with human needs, we risk finding ourselves in a marketing world devoid of emotion, serendipity, and magic, where we lose sight of the art behind the science, the very essence of a brand and what it can do for a consumer.

This book will give you a new way to reach and engage your customers across screens. Using case studies from Fortune 500 companies, as well as agile small and medium-sized businesses, we'll share how companies are taking a consumer-centric perspective to develop multi-screen marketing strategies. We will focus on seven distinct calls to action to take your business forward in the multi-screen world:

1. Meet the People behind the Screens

2. Understand Your Customers' Decision Journey

3. Introducing Quality Social

4. Simplify Your Multi-Screen Content Strategy

5. Drive Efficiency by Targeting Consumer Needs, Not "Millennials and Moms"

6. Initiate Action with Seamless Experiences across Screens

7. Measure Consumer Metrics, Not Device Metrics

First, we'll introduce you to a group of people you may actually think you know well: your customers. In the digital age, more and more businesses ignore their hard-earned knowledge of their customers in favor of the screens they use. *Meet the Screens*, the first thought leadership study we conducted together in 2011, was designed to answer this big question. We'll use Jungian archetypes to identify the unique ways consumers relate to each screen and reveal best practices for crafting campaigns for mobile phones, televisions, computers, and tablets. We will also provide a business case from a small start-up company to illustrate how tapping into the unique relationship consumers share with each device can ultimately simplify multi-screen advertising campaigns.

If you've ever wondered why you look up consumer reviews after making a purchase, you'll want to read Chapter 3, "Know Your Customer's Decision Journey," which uses Microsoft's framework for consumer decision making to identify not just the dominant behaviors exhibited as consumers travel the path to purchase (e.g., looking up consumer reviews, using search), but also reveals their underlying needs and motivations at each stage. The Consumer Decision Journey framework outlines how consumers make purchase decisions across different industry verticals—consumer packaged goods, automotive, retail, and financial services. At each stage in these decision journeys, we identify which screens and what type of content will make people's purchase decisions easier, lead to actual purchases, and build closer connections to brands. At the core, this framework focuses on understanding consumer needs at each stage of the decision journey to drive more engaging and ultimately more effective marketing.

Through this framework, we'll zero in on the points where consumers experience friction, and then identify how marketers can smooth the way. Our case study illustrates how a simple insight about a customer's need in-store opened up a new business opportunity for a compelling start-up company. We'll also share how Microsoft is thinking about the ongoing transformation of the retail environment through deeper personalization and the increased enhancement of the real via touch screens, voice, and gesture.

"Introducing Quality Social," in Chapter 4 takes on the all-too-common business tactic of having a platform-based social media line item in a marketing budget without thinking through a strategy based on actual social behavior. Here, we'll introduce the idea of Quality Social and explain why your "quantity-over-quality" approach isn't working. We'll also explore niche networking post purchasing validation and social spider webbing as ways to activate quality social across platforms. We'll share an example of a powerhouse social media campaign from an innovative espresso machine manufacturer that harnessed the real power of social motivation without buying a single media impression.

"Consumers are in control" is a common maxim these days. And yet in our research, we've found that consumers don't actually *want* control: they want curation. And that's good for marketers, too, because it helps them simplify their content strategy. Chapter 5, "Simplify Your Multi-Screen Content Strategy," provides evidence that while consumers seek transparency from brands, they still rely on media to provide a finite, yet relevant set of choices. In other words, consumers want access to flight information, but they still want a pilot to fly the plane. We will share best practices for curating content using our Consumer Journey framework, and bring it to life through case studies from Bing and Volkswagen China.

Chapter 6 illustrates how to "Drive Efficiency by Targeting Consumer Needs, Not 'Millennials and Moms'." When marketers focus on consumer needs instead of standard demographics, they may find that suburban teenage boys have more in common with urban professional moms than they ever imagined. We will challenge traditional modes of consumer segmentation and targeting, and offer up multi-screen solutions that bring you closer to true personalization and relevance. We'll include an example from a major beauty brand who uses the Xbox platform to reach and engage a surprising audience segment with stellar results.

Chapter 7, "Initiate Action with Seamless Experiences Across Screens," highlights the importance of providing connected experiences across screens in order to drive purchase behavior. In what we call Quantum Pathways, 46 percent of consumers leap over time, space, and screens to achieve a goal.[3] They start an activity on one screen and continue it on another. This pathway is sequential and distinctly intent based; as a result, ease and productivity are paramount. We'll share ways brands can provide more unified experiences across computers, tablets, mobile phones, and even gaming consoles and why this is of critical importance from a consumer perspective. Additionally, we'll talk to a Microsoft engineer with a fascinating take on how the future of data exchange will create a new marketplace for consumers and brands, enabling more seamless and personalized interaction along the way.

Finally, Chapter 8, "Measure Consumer Metrics, Not Device Metrics," offers up a new way to frame media measurement: not by device but via the behavior and underlying motivations of the people we're actually measuring. We identify the importance of integrating consumer key performance indicators (KPIs) with marketer objectives to ensure our multi-screen campaigns deliver value to consumers, as well as to marketers.

The shift from manufactured primetime spots and static advertising placements to consumers engaging with content through multiple screens presents unprecedented opportunities. When our industry's focus shifts from tablets, mobile phones, and computers to the consumers who use them, we uncover meaningful patterns of human motivation. A deep understanding of these patterns enable marketers, business professionals, designers, and technologists to leverage the right screen with the right message in the right moment—subsequently bringing true utility to consumers, and in turn, deeper value for marketers.

CHAPTER 2

Meet the People behind the Screens

MARKET TO YOUR CUSTOMERS, NOT TO THEIR DEVICES

When we first formed the Consumer Insights team and started meeting with brands and agencies, one of the questions that came up repeatedly was whether it was okay to take an advertisement made for television and stream it across different screens. Most customers recognized the importance of expanding beyond television, but balked at the complexity and expense of creating different campaigns for the computer, mobile phone, and tablet. Or they simply didn't know where to start. Wearing our pragmatist hats, it seemed like a sensible thing to prioritize having a presence on multiple screens, even with a repurposed television advertisement. Being absent from the digital space wasn't a great option, and at least people would see the campaign and take in the message within the context of each different screen. But in our guts, we knew that this was a pretty blunt approach and overlooked some basic lessons we'd learned over the years.

First, you can't assume that consumers see televisions, computers, mobile phones, and tablets as interchangeable. Although we do some of the same things across these devices—watch video or search—you would never just swap out your mobile for your laptop. Each screen fulfills different needs in our lives, which made us realize that maybe these needs are worth paying attention to.

Second, the one-size-fits-all-screens approach elevates devices over content. Any creative agency would beg to differ if you insisted that advertising content is less important than the devices or channels that carry it. And, in fact, anyone who ever conducts creative testing will tell you that how the message is crafted is just as important, if not more, than where the message actually shows up. By assuming that a single advertisement can be streamed across any screen, we were walking right into the trap of being device led, rather than consumer led. We know that focusing more on the devices in consumers' lives instead of the lives of consumers makes it infinitely more challenging to connect people to brands and services.

Acquiescing wasn't a viable option, so we decided to tackle this challenge head on and launched a global insights study that, ironically, became known as *Meet the Screens*, an unintentionally device-first name. The first order of business was to move swiftly beyond understanding device usage to uncovering the different relationships consumers have with their televisions, computers, mobile phones, and tablets. To ensure that we were telling a truly global story, we decided to run the research in the United States, the U.K., Russia, China, and Saudi Arabia, and we included a wide span of age groups. At a basic level, we wanted to affirm that consumers—regardless of where they live, or how old they are— relate to each screen differently. We also wanted to understand how marketers could optimize their marketing on each device to capitalize on and tap into the distinct relationships consumers share with each screen.

One of the challenges that hit us immediately was how to get consumers to actually talk about their relationships with the screens in their lives. It's always really easy to get people to describe their behaviors (what they do), but it can be pretty challenging to get them to talk about emotional connections and relationships with inanimate (let alone animate!) objects. This challenge becomes even greater when you're talking to people from different countries and across different age groups. The way around this challenge was proposed by one of our favorite research guys, Ian Wright, who was with Ipsos OTX at the time. He had a lot of success using Carl Jung's archetypes as a way to get people to make emotional associations without actually talking about emotions—an inspired suggestion, as it turned out.

Without launching into a dissertation on Jung, it is worth explaining what archetypes are and how they work. Archetypes are basically personifications or symbols of all the core relationships that we have with ourselves, other people, and the world around us.[1] Jung identified archetypes that not only are the basis for psychoanalysis, but also the foundation of many classic books and movies, including *Star Wars*, *The Lord of the Rings* trilogy, and the Harry Potter series. You have the Hero—Luke Skywalker, Frodo, Harry Potter—who is on a journey of discovery about the world and ultimately himself. These Heroes are frequently bailed out by a Wizard—Obi-Wan Kenobi, Gandalf, Dumbledore—in times of distress, while being provoked by various Outlaws, supported by Lovers, and humored by Jesters. Transmitted into the world of marketing, archetypes can be used to build a brand identity, construct personas around target consumers, and, as we discovered, illuminate the core relationship that consumers share with their televisions, computers, mobile phones, and tablets.

As it turns out, our gut instincts were right. Consumers have very distinct relationships with each of these screens.

These distinctions mean that taking a single advertising execution and assuming it will work effectively on different screens is overly optimistic. At the very least, consumers will ignore advertising that "doesn't fit" or seems incompatible. At the very worst, placing advertising that is incongruous with a device can be irritating and disruptive, driving a wedge between consumers and brands. The opportunity for marketers lies in crafting advertising that taps into and enhances these unique consumer-screen relationships. It is far easier to stream into (or enhance) an existing, meaningful connection than to establish one from scratch or bump up against one that is already established and flourishing. The rest of this chapter will explain how marketers can do exactly this. We'll walk through the relationship consumers have with each screen, lay out how marketers can successfully deliver content to capitalize on these relationships, provide examples of marketing that does this well, and then discuss how this all plays out in a multi-screen world.

TELEVISION: THE JESTER AND EVERYMAN

When you think about it, television is like an old friend. It's been in our lives for decades (*and* decades . . . but let's not age ourselves), and for many of us (aging ourselves again!), it was our first and only screen. When we wake up in the morning or drag ourselves home after a busy day at work, the television is faithfully waiting to entertain and spend time with us. It's the screen we turn to when we want to wind down and have some respite from the complexity in our lives, in much the same way we catch up with friends over a beer to share a few laughs.

Fittingly, the two archetypes people associate with the television embody the core traits of a good friend: the Jester, a source of fun, laughter, and entertainment; and the Everyman, a reliable, easy-going, normal guy or girl. Not only can we relate easily to our old friend the television, it also happens to be pretty fun to have around. In fact, one of our respondents from the U.K. says, "It's someone to hang out with when there's no one else around . . . it keeps me company."

Some interesting nuances in the Jester/Everyman relationship emerge between countries and across age groups. For people in developed markets like the United States and the U.K., television is not just an old friend, but a trusted one. The default mode is to generally enjoy and be receptive to content on this screen. In Russia and China, television suffers from a legacy of state-controlled content, which has made people's relationship with this screen less open and guileless. While people still see television as an old friend, it is one that you keep at arm's length. This means that content on television is more likely to be questioned—or at least not unfailingly trusted. So, in these markets, television may not be the optimal screen for building close connections between consumers and brands. This isn't to say that all television advertising in China and Russia will immediately be viewed mistrustfully, but it is worth considering how to fold other, more trusted screens into advertising campaigns in these countries.

Similar patterns emerge when we look at different age groups. People over 40 have a very close relationship with their televisions—they are the high school friends that we still have cocktails with on Friday night. This close relationship has solidified through years of knowing each other and being exclusive friends. As a result, this age group is most likely to trust and be responsive to content, including advertising, on television. Taking in content on television is almost second nature. For people under 40, television is more like an old friend whom they've outgrown. They still love having television around, but there are so many more interesting, cooler screens out there. Unlike their older counterparts, this generation came of age in a two-screen world. And, for most of their lives, the computer has been a dominant presence alongside television. The implications for marketers are clear—if you want to reach people under 40, being solely focused on television means missing big opportunities to connect your brands and services to this age group in a meaningful way.

Nuances aside, if television is our Jester and Everyman, how do marketers ensure their advertising is congruent with what people seek from this screen? Let's start to answer this question using the old friend analogy. Imagine that it's been a pretty hectic day at work: you're tired, not feeling very switched on, and you just want to relax and share a few laughs with a good friend. You are looking for some effortless fun. But instead, the conversation turns to politics and your friend starts spouting esoteric, complicated nonsense. You go home feeling annoyed, wound-up, and irritated. A good night out shouldn't be such hard work! It's the same with television advertising. When you are looking to wind down and be entertained, you don't want to spend hours trying to decipher what an advertiser is telling you. You want to be able to drift seamlessly between your favorite show and the advertising, intuitively absorbing the stories and messages. Who wants to be around an old friend who is hard work? If television advertising isn't conveying a clear message, entertaining us on some level, and eliciting an emotional reaction, then it's not really doing its job.

If we were to go through every television advertisement that taps into the Jester and Everyman archetypes, we could probably fill this book with great case studies. As an industry, we've generally nailed television advertising. So, we're going to be forced to cherry-pick a bit. The two television advertisements that we highlight here do a particularly brilliant job of tapping into the Jester and Everyman relationship we share with television. This is advertising that is exceptionally intuitive; it entertains, and connects with us emotionally.

The creative agency BBDO's Carleton Beer ad juxtaposes a slow-motion bar scene featuring a few guys enjoying their beer and playing darts against a tenor singing opera in the background. The surprising combination creates effortless drama in an everyday scene, and humor in what would otherwise be a fairly pedestrian day at the bar. The ad brilliantly puts the brand in the midst of a relatable mini-drama without asking the consumer to do any work.

On the other side of the coin, Unilever's Dove Real Beauty television commercials create some of the most relatable content in the beauty industry. The expressions of the women featured when they see their perceptions of themselves versus others in the sketch artist's designs is quite simply some of the most emotional and compelling content on television, so resonant that even in a 30-second spot, it's nearly impossible not to tear up a bit. The ad strums the right emotional chords in just a short amount of time.

THE COMPUTER: THE SAGE

In the not so distant past, if we noticed a weird rash on our leg, we'd consult a medical book. Trip planning was managed through travel agents, and niggling questions were answered by asking a smart friend or turning to the encyclopedia. With the advent of the computer and the Internet, all of these traditional routes to getting advice, information, and answers are practically obsolete.

The computer has become a reference library, doctor, encyclopedia, book store, and clever friend/relative all rolled into one. In effect, it's our Sage. Sages are intellectual guides who bestow the gift of knowledge to help us navigate the pathways of life. They're the people we turn to when we want help or information to make us better, smarter, and more competent. Parents, older siblings, teachers, bosses, and—if you live in New York—your therapist, are all classic Sages. Without Sages, we'd stumble around blindly, making mistakes and learning things the hard way. When you think about the computer in Sage terms, it is clear what a powerful and multi-dimensional role this screen plays in our lives. Computers have become something close to an authority figure. This becomes especially clear when we hear consumers talk about being "beholden to their computers" and "dependent on them" to get things done. There is power in something that helps make us smarter, more competitive, and productive. In fact, a consumer in Singapore describes her computer like this: "It's my guardian angel . . . when I'm not sure what to do, I consult my laptop."

Although people across geographies and different age groups all see their computers as Sages, the intensity of their relationship varies. In Russia and China, the computer is trusted above all other screens, while television is trusted more in the United States and the U.K. Why the discrepancy?

As we know, the legacy of state-controlled television content in Russian and China has bred lingering mistrust, but with the computer there is a sense of having much more personal control over what content is viewed and consumed. Even though we know governments block certain websites or sources of information, the Internet is a pretty big place, and people can find back routes and new ways to access the content they seek. With television, you get what you get. In Russia and China, marketers miss an immense opportunity if they aren't folding the computer into their advertising plans. When you are trying to convince people to bring your brands and services into their lives, it can be very powerful to land this message on a screen where people go to get trusted information and advice.

When we turn to the different age groups, we see that younger people feel closer to their computers than they do to television. It's not that they don't trust television content, but computers simply play a more important role in their lives. As we discussed earlier, people under 40 were born in a dual screen world, and the computer has been an integral part of their lives since they were children. And when they have to choose between their computers and televisions, computers win out because they just *do* more than televisions. They can be a source of entertainment, but they are also their Sages—where they go when they want information, advice, and to be productive. This isn't to say that people over 40 don't similarly appreciate the broader utility of their computers, but they still feel closer to the television because it has been in their lives longer. So, the upshot for marketers is that having advertising on laptops is key to reaching the younger generation; they still watch television, but the computer is a powerful screen for capturing their attention, mindshare, and focus.

We're not really going to stir up a lot of controversy when we stand on our soapbox, proclaiming the importance of digital advertising on the computer. A lot of heads are likely nodding when we emphasize the importance of the computer as a means to connect with younger generations and with people in countries like Russia and China. We're at a point in our industry's evolution where there is broad acknowledgment that digital advertising is important. Given this, it's heartening that we've made great strides in digital advertising (banners for miracle anti-aging products aside). But a lot of our focus remains fixed on advertising that taps into the features and functions of the computer—search, display, video—at the expense of leveraging the deeper relationship that people have with this screen. When you shift focus and start to think about the power of the computer as the Sage, the way we view the computer within an advertising context changes.

The computer is the screen that "owns" intellectual engagement, information, data, advice, and productivity; it helps people feel knowledgeable and better equipped to make good decisions.

There is a lot of power and potential in the Sage that we can harness as marketers. On a very basic level, great display advertising on laptops and desktops should engage people—this isn't the place for passive messaging. Sages demand attention and focus.

The computer is also a place where brands can step in to help people be good decision makers by providing the right facts at the right moment, or dispense advice so that people feel armed with the knowledge they need to solve a problem or address an issue. These are all very powerful roles for brands and services. Life is complicated, so brands that can help us navigate through this complexity by arming us with information and knowledge are in a very powerful position. This doesn't have to be complicated, overwrought advertising. It can be as simple as providing shopping checklists to help people find ingredients for a new dish that contains a food manufacturer's new product—or a mortgage interest rate calculator integrated into a financial services advertisement. When you think about taking a television advertisement and placing it on the computer, it is probably one of the greatest underutilizations of this screen's immense advertising potential.

While the notion of the computer as Sage isn't widely known among marketers, many still implicitly understand that this screen delivers productivity, knowledge, and advice. This means that we can point to a number of great digital campaigns that tap into the computer's role as Sage. And it isn't just the big marketing campaigns from Fortune 500 companies that have delivered best practice display advertising; we've found some smaller, independent businesses that deserve to be spotlighted here. In fact, digital advertising on the computer and mobile phone is perhaps the greatest democratizing influence in advertising: if done well, you don't necessarily need outsize budgets to pull it off.

We've included an example from a small start-up business, Yezi Tea, further on to illustrate just how powerful digital media can be on the computer when leveraged as The Sage.

THE MOBILE: THE LOVER

Have you ever lost your mobile phone, had it stolen, or (this may put me squarely in the minority) dropped it in a toilet? Perhaps you have been spared this moment of panic or, in the case of the toilet, indignity. For the rest of us, it is strangely paralyzing when our mobile disappears or stops working—*what am I going to do?* For many people, losing their mobile phone is worse than misplacing their wallet. And we're not just overly attached to our mobile phones; we feel very proprietary about them, too. When people borrow our mobile to make a call, we watch and wait for them to hurry up and hand it back. Mobile phones are intensely personal and private devices. It almost feels like a minor violation when people start trawling through our mobile phones, even if we're (pretty) sure they don't contain illicit texts or incriminating photos. So it makes a lot of sense that people choose the Lover archetype to describe their relationship with their mobile phone. Lovers stir up our emotions and connect with us deeply, personally, and meaningfully. Time and time again in our research, we hear people very passionately describe the role the mobile plays in their life: it's "like my heartbeat," the "center of my life," and "a part of me."[2]

How did mobile phones become our Lovers? To begin with, they are always physically close to us. When you go to bed at night, the last thing you probably look at is your mobile phone, and it may be the first thing you grab in the morning (perhaps to the distress of the other Lover in your life). Mobile content is often very personal and meaningful: photos of family and friends;

sentimental texts; people's contact details; and saved e-mails that make us feel good when we read them. Even the way we customize our mobiles is reflective of who we are and what matters to us: a photo of our child, dog, or partner as our wallpaper and a song or sound we like as our ringtone. And, if we think about the basic purpose of a mobile phone, it enables us to connect with the people we care about through calling, texting, and e-mailing. From content to function, the mobile phone embodies the Lover.

The geographic differences and nuances between age groups that we observed around people's relationships with their televisions and computers do not exist with the mobile phone. To begin with, mobiles as smartphones haven't been in our lives that long, particularly compared to the decades we've spent with televisions and computers. So, our relationship with our Lovers is relatively new—perhaps explaining some of the intensity. Because of this newness, there aren't legacies of content control, or the tedium of knowing each other too long that color our relationship with television. In fact, the deep, personal bond people share with their mobile phones makes them trust content on this device more than any other, with the very notable exception of advertising content. The very nature of this close relationship can make advertising feel like an unwelcome intruder.

Here's an analogy to bring the point home. Imagine you are sitting in a restaurant in Rome on a lovely romantic holiday with your partner. In the midst of enjoying a cheap but great bottle of red and a delicious plate of pasta, a violinist walks up to your table and starts playing a song you don't like. A wonderful, intimate moment ruined! You silently implore the guy to leave and even slip him some euros hoping he'll take the hint, but the mood of the meal is lost. You are left feeling angry with the restaurant and even forget that the meal was actually delicious. The musician is the equivalent of the wrong advertising on a mobile phone—invasive and unwelcome. The private and intimate relationship that we share with our mobiles means that advertising that isn't respectful of this bond can raise our ire against the brands that invade this personal space. A wonderful, intimate connection, spoiled!

Now, take this same romantic meal in Rome: the wine, pasta, and lovely ambience. The same guy walks up and plays a song on his violin that happens to be your all-time favorite, perhaps the song you danced to at your wedding. This intimate moment becomes more poignant, magical, and memorable. And every year, you make a pilgrimage to this same restaurant, hoping to recapture this lovely evening. These are the sorts of connections we yearn to make between consumers and brands. When mobile advertising is personal and meaningful, it can be far more powerful than advertising on any other screen. Creating an intimate moment between people and your brands through advertising that respects this "Lover" relationship is a potent marketing opportunity.

How can marketers create mobile advertising that is the equivalent of the violinist playing a meaningful, moment-enhancing song? On a basic level, application or app-based advertising is a simple and effective way to ensure that advertising will be personal and relevant. For an app to appear on a mobile phone, the user must find it and choose to download it. It's unlikely we'll download an app that is meaningless, irrelevant, or uninteresting. We've picked it because it resonates with us on some level, and we've made a personal choice to put it on our mobile phone, this most proprietary of devices. With app-based advertising, you already have some assurance that your content won't be viewed as an unwelcome intruder since it's been invited in.

But marketers need to do more than just avoid being unwelcome intruders—that's a pretty low bar. Our ultimate goal should be to create truly powerful mobile phone advertising that connects people to brands in a more profound way. To accomplish this, advertising on the mobile must be personal, meaningful, or helpful on some level, and it must elicit a positive emotional reaction. One of our biggest challenges as marketers is that we've tended to view mobile phones in an incredibly rational and tactical way—driven, again, by an overarching focus on the features and function of this device. It's portable, so let's use it to send coupons, promotional deals, or price comparison apps that people can pick up in-store.

None of this is wrong, particularly if the coupons, deals, and price comparisons are for brands, products, or stores that people like; at least this approach covers the need for personalized content. But as marketers, we're missing an immense opportunity to tap into the emotional connection people have with their mobiles: the Lover relationship. We should be striving to land content that is personal but also triggers a positive emotional response, which all good branded advertising should do anyway. Mobile advertising that places your brand in the role of personal goal facilitator is one straightforward strategy: a calorie counter to help with weight loss; shopping lists that automatically update based on knowledge of product usage; recipe ideas that cater to health issues we're managing. Even though these aren't lofty, big ideas, they are personal and customized to the individual, and they help people manage things that are important to them, such as health and well-being, productivity, and being in control. This is truly harnessing the power of the mobile phone.

Finding great mobile advertising that does justice to the Lover is not as easy as finding strong digital advertising that capitalizes on the Sage relationship people have with their computers. The vast majority of content that marketers place on mobiles tends to be impersonal—a banner ad for a dating site that pops up when I watch a video (even though I'm married and have a child)—or deeply unemotional—geolocation-driven advertising that is helpful, but doesn't exactly connect with me on a meaningful level. There are, however, a few really powerful examples of great mobile advertising that are either so deeply personal that they trigger an emotional response or create an instant emotional connection by fulfilling a need or motivation that is important. There is one in particular that we'd like to highlight—Pretty in My Pocket (PRIMP)—which appears at the end of Chapter 3. It is deeply grounded in consumer needs and highly personal, truly best practice mobile marketing.

THE TABLET: THE EXPLORER

Like any relationship, the ones we have with our screens can evolve over time as they go from being new, fresh, and exciting to more established and mature. When we first spoke to people about their relationship with their tablets, these screens had been around for under a year in terms of mass availability and ownership. Tablets were such exciting things! They almost felt magical to people—or like superheroes (as one guy in China proclaimed)—simply because they just do so much. You could read restaurant reviews on the digital version of *Food and Wine*, e-mail some friends and invite them to try the hot new featured restaurant, find the restaurant on a map, book the reservations, take photos of you and your friends at the restaurant, post the photos to a social site, and create a photo album to record this wonderful night—all on one device!

In these early days, people characterized their relationship with their tablets as Wizards, a magical screen that fulfills our wishes and desires on command. Like marketers, people's connection with tablets was grounded primarily in what this device could *do*—its functions and features. As portable as a mobile phone but with a bigger screen, it seemed far more adaptable and useful. But given this magical aura, it was really hard to figure out how to land marketing on this screen. And, in many ways, it was almost premature to think about marketing on tablets because three years ago, we hadn't even begun to master advertising on mobile phones. Why add to the complexity?

Fast-forward three years. Tablets are now ubiquitous. No one stops you at the airport to ask you about this magical device propped on your lap. Tablets have become a seamless part of our lives: they sit on our coffee tables, show up at meetings, are faithful travel companions, and even make the occasional appearance in our kitchens when we're trying out new recipes. Our relationship with our tablets has matured and mellowed, and we've settled into a new phase of our journey together.

As we all know, when relationships mature, the magic starts to recede and gets replaced with something more substantial and enduring—or so we hope! In the case of people's relationship with their tablets, this is exactly what has happened. The Wizard has hung up his wand and hat, and a new archetype has settled in his place: the Explorer. Explorers are our guides on voyages of discovery, taking us to new places, satisfying our quest for finding interesting and exciting things, and helping satiate our curiosity about the world around us. While tablets may not take us to the tops of mountains and across raging rivers, they guide us on all sorts of virtual journeys through new, interesting, and interactive content. We can cover miles of digital territory or go deep and explore one piece of engaging and exciting content, all facilitated by our tablets.

The tactile nature of tablets also provides a sense of immediacy and engagement on these content journeys; one swipe of the hand can take us to a magazine to read content, expand a fascinating photo, and activate a video that offers an immersive, transporting experience. One of our favorite quotes from our 2013 *Cross-Screen Engagement* research, part two of *Meet the Screens*, captures this sentiment perfectly: "My tablet is like a ship that takes me to new places. There's an ocean of things to discover."[3]

Like mobile phones, the tablet is still a relatively new screen in our lives, so we don't see big differences in the intensity or substance of people's relationship with their tablets across geographies or age groups. But unlike mobile phones, tablets aren't particularly personal devices. You may bristle when your partner or child picks up your mobile and starts playing around with it, but the tablet is much more a community device. While some families have more than one tablet, many share one—with varying degrees of conflict—which gets picked up, used, and put down by different family members throughout the day. So there isn't the same singular need for personalized, bespoke, and emotionally engaging content on the tablet as there is on the mobile phone.

Given this, marketers should not use the tablet as just another screen on which to land advertising. Static, two-dimensional content, a banner ad, a promotional offer, even a video, all profoundly underexploit the potential of the tablet and do very little to tap into people's desire to embark on content journeys on this screen. This sort of advertising is like taking a trip to your front stoop. You don't really get very far or discover anything interesting.

The tablet as Explorer flags up endless opportunities for marketers to drive deep immersion and engagement with brands. People in an exploratory mind-set aren't looking for superficial or quick journeys; they want to uncover uncharted territory, discover exciting things, and go deeper into what fascinates them. Inviting people on a lengthy, exciting journey with your brand can often be the spark that starts a fulfilling relationship or solidifies an existing one. This doesn't mean that marketers need to build complex campaigns with lots of different creative executions to successfully connect their brands with consumers on tablets. It's about layering content, enabling people to dive in and out of different experiences and to go deep into others. This could be as simple as having the equivalent of a print ad with active links embedded in it that enable people to explore different elements of the content in more detail—the images, brand logo, or key words in the copy.

Imagine consumers landing on a recipe site, but instead of having a big collection of recipes to scroll through or sort, they can move swiftly from reading a Pad Thai recipe to clicking on a link that takes them to a microsite describing the cuisine of Thailand. Additional links show videos of chefs preparing Thai food and descriptions of ingredients and flavors with rich, evocative imagery. Not only does this elevate the classic, static digital recipe experience by making it interactive, interesting, and informative, but the brand that drives this exploratory experience is playing a starring role educating, helping, and engaging the consumer. As consumers become increasingly inured to digital advertising, particularly traditional formats that feel intrusive and irrelevant, the tablet becomes the perfect tableau for launching advertising experiences that consumers can opt into and move through in a way that suits their needs and allows them to access what they want, when they want it.

There isn't a wealth of great tablet advertising to share. In fact, one of the biggest confounding factors preventing us from tapping into the huge potential of tablet advertising is our tendency to throw the tablet in the same category as the mobile because they are both portable. Once again, oversimplification by function and feature gets in the way of effective advertising.

The mobile and tablet have very little in common except for the fact that you can carry them around. Once you understand the critical differences in how people relate to these two devices, you would be hard pressed to consider using the same advertising on each of these screens. Consumers don't want to go on journeys of exploration on their mobile phones—the screens are too small to cultivate an immersive experience, and time spent on this device tends to be pretty measured. As a result, consumers want meaningful, actionable advertising on their mobiles. On the tablet, consumers seek out serendipitous content that sparks discovery and investigation, and satisfies their desire to find new, interesting things.

Given this device conflation, we had to work hard to find best practice tablet advertising to share. One fruitful route to finding great digital content is through digital magazines. Magazines contain a lot of inspirational, creative content that fits squarely in the realm of the Explorer and can easily be co-opted for advertising on the tablet. But, how does this look when a business actually applies it? Our case study illustrates how one small company will choose where to put their focus in order to accomplish their key marketing goals out of the gate.

CASE STUDY: YEZI TEA

In 2013, Meiqin Weng and Boris Musa founded Yezi Tea, an online-only tea distribution company that brings premium Chinese teas to the United States and Canada. Weng grew up in the Fujian province, where oolong and black teas first originated in the Wuyi mountains. In fact, the English word *tea* actually comes from the Min Nan language in the Fujian region. When Weng came to the United States 10 years ago, she was disappointed to find that most teas sold in stores were of an inferior quality to those she had grown up with in China. While she had relationships with tea farmers back home, she wasn't sure how to get their harvest to the North American tea-sipping public. When she met Boris Musa, an experienced e-commerce architect with a taste for Chinese tea, she knew she was onto something. Musa and Weng built Yezi, which means "leaf" in Chinese, in order to bring the great Fujian teas of Weng's childhood from the misty hills of Fujian to the tea cups of North American consumers.

"First and foremost, it's an education challenge," Weng explained. "When you are served tea here in America, it often contains artificial flavors—like fruits or even cinnamon—which masks the true flavor and quality of the tea. That quality, when you can actually taste it, is inferior . . . often sour, with expired or crushed tea leaves. Most consumers don't know the difference."

Until they taste Yezi tea, that is. Because we conducted our interview over a cup of black tea (or, more accurately, "red tea," as it's known in China), I can attest that even my preservative-stunted American palate can discern that Weng and Musa have a terrific product. As one recent tea reviewer said about a Yezi master-grade white tea, "This tea explodes out of the cup. The fragrance is incredible as soon as the hot water hits, suffusing the air with flowers tightly enclosed within their pre-spring buds. Wow."[4]

But aside from charming in-the-know tea bloggers, Weng and Musa needed to find their audience. How does a two-person company with an excellent product, a direct connection to the source, and a sophisticated infrastructure system drive demand and find leads without an Amazon-sized marketing budget? Similar to what Starbucks did for coffee in the 1990s, they first needed to educate potential customers on what makes a truly satisfying cup of tea. To do just that, Weng and Musa deployed the device that people turn to for knowledge: The Sage. While their site is optimized for mobile phones and tablets, Musa knew that in the first stage of his business, he needed to focus on desktops and laptops as the primary screens to help them find and educate their audience.

Musa set up an advanced customer tracking system and started to build demand by targeting tea drinkers through search campaigns and social media. Both he and Weng felt confident that tea lovers just needed to try the product—and they would be hooked. To get customers in their virtual door, they offered up a free tea sample and shipped it quickly.

Even more important, however, they wanted to build an opt-in e-mail mailing list they could leverage to start educating customers about the quality of their tea over time. That's right—*e-mail*. It's still one of the most personal and powerful online marketer tools. According to Musa, he sees 50 percent open rates and 20 percent click-through rates (on average) from his subscription list, most of which resulted from their initial free sample offer, compelling creativity, and a closely targeted audience. The value of this list to Weng and Musa is that it lets them control messaging and gives an initial high-quality impression that draws users to a website that elaborates on the quality theme and ultimately develops and nurtures a more educated consumer over time.

Like all start-ups, there were some good lessons along the way. "We had a free sample offer that we thought was very generous," Musa said. "But we got all sorts of complaints that paying three dollars for shipping and handling for a free sample was unreasonable. Well, now we know that people don't see any value in shipping, so we should build free shipping offers instead of percentage-off offers."

Musa and Weng continued to educate customers by tapping into the Sage mind-set with videos featuring Weng on YeziTea .com about how to properly prepare tea, as well as in-depth profiles of the farmers who grow the tea they sell. The computer lends itself to these interactions because it's a place where most consumers have years of experience conducting research; they're less focused on the device and subsequently more likely to lend their attention to deeper content. As a result, the medium itself recedes and leaves room for the content—and subsequent learning—to come to the forefront.

Musa said most traffic is currently coming from desktop computers, though he's seeing an increase in tablet and mobile usage. As he gains more repeat customers, he expects their comfort levels in ordering through tablet and mobile will only increase—especially as the relationships Yezi builds with these customers become less about education over time and more about more experiential exploration on tablets and personal utility on mobile phones.

Focusing on desktops and laptops in the initial stages of their business, rather than getting too caught up in building mobile apps and tablet campaigns, has enabled Weng and Musa to focus on the basics first: identifying and building an educated audience. Weng spends more of her time providing high levels of customer service: quick shipment, close monitoring of orders, and staying on top of available touchpoints in order to reinforce the positioning of their brand as a premium offering. Close monitoring also helps them glean which segments respond to their tests best. Weng and Musa heavily leverage niche tea communities such as Steepster and networks like Reddit in order to monitor chatter about their brand and stay in touch with customers who have questions.

"People ask things like 'What's the difference between loose leaf and others?' 'How do I properly preserve the tea?' 'How long can I keep it before I need to throw it out?'" Weng said. They can also monitor campaigns quickly to adjust targeting, search investment, and word of mouth—just as they learned to adjust the lack of a shipping and handling charge based on social media comments.

Musa's philosophy in running an online business is the inverse of how most food and beverage manufacturers approach it—and this may be the secret to their future success. Musa is automating everything from shipping to customer relationship management so he and Weng can focus on the quality of the teas they get from farmers in China—where the real soul of their business lies.

"Most tea companies get their products from large, fully automated, export-oriented plantations, where every step of farming is done by machines," Musa said. "I want our tea to be hand-crafted, unique, to originate from small farms where people take pride in their teas and strive for constant perfection. We prefer a human to pick the product, but we can pack and ship the product with a machine. I would rather have final distribution automated so we can bring it to our customers quickly, but use people to do the human things."

Weng and Musa are on year one in their start-up adventure. They expect to expand to additional channels, including a mobile phone app, as they continue to build their subscription list and fine-tune their audience target. In Chapter 4, we'll take a look at how espresso machine manufacturer La Marzocco, a company that's recently celebrated its 90th anniversary, has taken the next step and leveraged digital channels across screens to build a niche network around their product. In the meantime, we'll be following Yezi Tea to see where they go next (see Figure 2.1).

"I'm very particular about tea," said Weng. "If I won't drink it, I'm not going to sell it. . . . I want to give people an opportunity to have a real experience through tea, the same experience that's been thriving for a thousand years in China."

Figure 2.1   Yezi Tea Website with Sage-Like Information

MARKETER IMPLICATIONS

When it comes to crafting campaigns within the context of each device, we have a few key takeaways to keep in mind.

First, tap into the core relationship that consumers have with each screen to truly deliver multi-screen campaigns. This is very definitively not about landing a single campaign across different devices. That's like plastering every surface with an advertisement because these surfaces exist. It's also not about exploiting the features and functions of each device, which can lead to advertising that is fundamentally disconnected from consumers. Rather, marketers need to uncover the relationship between consumers and devices that defines not just how they use these devices, but how they use them to fulfill needs, goals, and motivations: to make smarter, more informed decisions; to connect with loved ones; to investigate content to satisfy curiosity; or to just have fun and be entertained. It helps to identify which screens to engage (there is no need to have every screen engaged to be multi-screen—you want the right ones) and *how* to engage consumers across each screen.

Second, know the archetypes for each screen and play to their strengths. Be the Everyman/Jester on television and gaming consoles: keep your message accessible; tell emotional stories; and build your brand and appeal to consumers' sense of fun. Be the Sage on the computer: provide deeper information, including reviews, ratings, facts, and authoritative content from experts and trusted sources to help consumers make faster, better decisions; facilitate analysis and make it easy for consumers to compare and contrast; and help consumers "close the deal."

Be the Lover on the mobile: deliver content that feels personal and meaningful; support consumers and make sure you're adding value, not interrupting them; facilitate personal connection and foster a feeling of belonging; and capitalize on the love connection between consumers and their mobile phones by landing branded content that elicits emotional—not just rational—responses.

Be the Explorer on the tablet: take consumers to new places; entice them and appeal to their sense of curiosity; tell stories by layering different types of content, including embedded links that lead to different narrative pathways, videos that enrich the story, or images that can be manipulated and explored; give consumers control of the discovery experience, but curate the content so you don't overwhelm them.

Truly effective advertising is not a one-size-fits-all proposition. In the future, the best campaigns will take full advantage of the different relationships that consumers have with screens and the archetypes they embody. The number of media consumers is growing rapidly, especially in emerging markets—and so is the number of screens we use. So it's more important than ever for marketers to create and tailor their messaging to be most relevant—and for consumers to be most receptive—depending on what screen they're with at the time. This is the foundation for successful multi-screen marketing.

The next step is to understand how consumers use these screens in combination. And while that may seem an overwhelming proposition, it's critical that marketers figure it out. We contend that all these screens don't limit a consumer's attention span; they multiply it. The relationships that marketers have with consumers can be deepened and enhanced *because of* the number of screens in their lives. As marketers, we need to use this knowledge to hone how screen-specific messages can work in unison in a multi-screen environment for maximum effect. We'll explore cross-screen engagement, including simultaneous, sequential, and separate multi-screening, in upcoming chapters.

CHAPTER 3

Know Your Customers' Decision Journey

USE SCREENS TO FACILITATE DECISION MAKING

In the writing world, whether in journalism or other storytelling disciplines, there's a mantra invoked time and time again: *know your audience*. And, it's pretty old news—something we've been honing since the very first hunter-gatherer learned to play to his audience over an open fire. And yet since digital came into our lives, it's a mantra that seems to have disappeared—or at least, it's been obfuscated with an obsession over the devices people use, rather than the actual living, breathing human beings that use them. It shouldn't be about what Xbox *can* do, it's about what consumers *need* Xbox to do.

Despite all the current hand-wringing about what will become of our short attention spans now that we're constantly connected through technology, human DNA hasn't changed just because pixels have come into our lives. Sure, our expectations for convenience, access to information, and utility have increased, but our essential needs, the same needs our grandmothers and great-grandmothers had before them, still run deep.

Seven in 10 people globally say their digital devices have brought them closer to brands.[1] So the opportunities to use screens to facilitate customer relationships are immense. But in order for businesses to use devices in ways that are both more functionally useful and emotionally resonant with consumers, we need to tap into two things: the foundational needs of our audience and the process by which they make decisions along their path to purchase. In this chapter, we're going to share a core framework that has enabled us to get a better understanding of consumers within our device-mad world: The Consumer Decision Journey.

In 2011, we partnered with OTX, a division within Ipsos founded by Shelley Zalis. Researcher and consumer insights expert Maury Giles had developed a compelling methodology that not only identifies the stages of consumer decision making along the path to purchase, but also the influencers across screens and the needs-states of consumers as they pass through each stage. While this method had never been used for media research before, we thought it would be particularly interesting to leverage it to light up how consumers were using digital platforms and traditional media, while identifying points in the journey where consumers were not being well served. These points of friction are essential to understand because they reveal opportunities for us to provide what consumers need in order to continue their journey, ultimately purchase goods and services, and even (ideally) become loyal users of a brand. And, of course, it's useful to Microsoft that our engineers can build platforms and solutions that enable these connections between marketers and consumers.

While there are nuances by vertical and category, we find that there are five consistent stages across the decision journey. And digital channels play a role in each stage. The first is what we call Open to Possibility.

The Open to Possibility stage is almost a pre-awareness phase; consumers may not have begun actively looking for a product or service, but they are slowly becoming aware of an emerging need or desire. This is where a psychological phenomenon called selective perception kicks in: while I may not be scouring *Consumer Reports* for a new car quite yet, I've seen a few ads for hybrid SUVs and am starting to notice more of these cars on my way to work. Eventually, it seems everyone has a hybrid SUV. Of course, this doesn't mean there are more hybrids on the road than the day before; I'm just more prone to notice them. Lo and behold, this desire bubbles up to the surface—do I need a more fuel-efficient car?—and I'm onto the second stage of the Consumer Decision Journey known as Decision to Buy or Change.

The Decision to Buy or Change kicks in when a consumer decides to try a new, different product that aligns with an emerging need, or replenish an existing product or service. With a habitual purchase, the catalyst for action is typically replenishing something that has run out. This stage can be triggered by an advertisement, a suggestion from a friend, or a life event. For example, having a baby will trigger a new car purchase for couples who want a bigger backseat for the car seat, the diaper bag, and all the other paraphernalia that comes with a deceptively small new member of the family.

That brings us to the third stage of the journey: Evaluating. This is the traditional research stage of the journey, where consumers will roll up their sleeves and start to gather information about the products in their consideration set. The almighty Internet has enabled consumers to get access to more information before making purchases than ever before. For considered and high-priced categories, this can be a lengthy and intense process involving a lot of online research, and reading expert and other consumer opinions. For habitual, everyday purchases, it might involve simply making a grocery list and checking the ingredients of a few recipes online.

When consumers have narrowed their consideration set, they enter the fourth stage: Shopping. Shopping can happen either online or in a brick and mortar environment; the way consumers approach it is dependent on the category. For expensive products like cars and flat screen TVs, consumers typically go into the retail environment ready to transact: they've done their research, and they know what they want. But for personal care and grocery products, consumers enjoy browsing and getting some "me time" as they check off items on their list and explore the retail environment at their leisure. This may seem counterintuitive, but we've found that consumers enjoy the retail experience for things they buy on a regular basis because there's less pressure to buy from salespeople and the lower price points means there's little risk involved.

But it doesn't end with the transaction. The last stage in the Consumer Decision Journey is Experiencing. This is the stage where consumers actually use the product or service they've bought—and hope that it meets their expectations. Experiencing involves all their associations with the product and how whether it delivers against these benefits and features when actually used. And, critically, this phase is not just about trying and liking a product, it's also about having others validate that you made a smart decision. Experiencing is a critical place where marketers need to drive loyalty and advocacy. After all, one consumer's experience can be another's Open to Possibility as brand advocates share and recommend what they like to new consumers.

Our journey research is unique in that we not only show what influences consumers along the journey, we also show what needs these influencers fulfill and on which screen. We accomplish this by asking a series of questions that place the influencers within the context of a consumer need-state. These needs are critical guideposts, helping us understand what content people seek to help them make decisions. In this chapter, we'll focus on four specific consumer needs.

The first is the need for personalization. From a consumer perspective, this is all about how a product might fit into one's life. Personalization can be as simple as seeing an ad on television that shows a family like mine enjoying conversation over cereal, or as sophisticated as using permissioned data to suggest a type of cereal that my family might really like based on my personal preferences and kids' allergies.

The second need is on the opposite end of the spectrum: validation. If personalization is all about what works for an individual, validation focuses on the group; it's about getting feedback and the wisdom of crowds. If you've ever looked up a review after you've bought an item to see what others think (are they as satisfied as I am? are others annoyed by that feature, too?), then you've experienced this need-state. Humans are social animals after all, and knowing what others think about the decisions we make is an important part of our decision-making process. Validation can also happen when consumers see products or services they like played back in the media. Seeing a woman on TV with beautiful hair, who is satisfied with her Finesse shampoo, can make me feel good that I use Finesse, too. The validation need-state is especially important to drive loyalty and advocacy through social behaviors—more on that in Chapter 4.

The third need-state is enrichment. Enrichment is actually a need that is relatively well-served through advertising, though not necessarily across screens. This is the more emotive part of your brain kicking in; it's all about communicating the essence or feel of a product. Television has traditionally done this very well, giving consumers a general and more emotive understanding of products and services. For example, beauty ads featuring models who have long, lustrous hair may evoke a sense that a shampoo brand will produce the same magnificent effect on all of us. We don't need a lot of facts here, just a clear emotional connection with the brand.

On the opposite side of enrichment sits information. This is just the facts, ma'am—the more rational part of our brains. Consumers need information about products and services in order to understand ingredients if they have an allergy, or specific features and benefits (do I want that flat screen with the LED 8000 or something else?). Information is a key component of the Evaluating stage of the Consumer Decision Journey, and yet many marketers serve up the general—enrichment—rather than the specific here. We also find that it's critical that marketers start giving consumers more cloud-based tools to compare and contrast product specs and benefits as they get close to making their decision.

What does this have to do with multi-screen marketing? It's simple, really. Read any marketing blog or go to any industry conference, and you're likely to hear "mobile first" as a new and disruptive theme. Mobile-first, while meant to be a provocative way to get this (still) emerging and essential channel to the forefront of traditional media planning, is just as problematic as a TV-first strategy. So instead of mobile-first (or any device-first strategy for that matter), we want to think *consumer-first*. Sometimes mobile technology will service your customers' needs, and sometimes it won't. The Consumer Decision Journey framework helps us know exactly when to use mobile and when to save our hard-earned marketing dollars for something else.

In the sections below, we'll share what we know based on our Consumer Decision Journey research by category, so you can jump to the section that's most relevant to your business. Each section contains key findings, including the top influencers and the screens that help facilitate decision making at each stage. This framework will give you a good place to start, but you'll want to layer in what you know about your own customers' behavior as well. And if you don't think you know enough, just ask them. As we'll share in Chapter 7, consumers are usually more than willing to share their habits if they know they'll get some value out of it: better service, offers, and deals, or simply more relevant interactions with a brand.

We'll close the chapter with a case study from the founder of a small start-up that shows how identifying a core consumer need along her decision journey not only helped identify the best screen for the job, but also revealed an entirely new business model. If you don't want to take a deeper dive into the categories below, we recommend jumping right to the Pretty in My Pocket Case Study later in this chapter.

THE CONSUMER DECISION JOURNEY: RETAIL

Two major themes emerge from our study *The Consumer Decision Journey: Retail*. The first is a blurring between the digital and the physical retail environments. While many retailers still separate brick and mortar from online retail channels, consumers see the two as connected, and they expect to feel that connection throughout their decision journey. Accessing circulars online and then bringing deals and coupons into the store, reading consumer reviews while at the shelf, and connecting back with a retailer through online channels if questions arise are all commonplace activities. But they're hardly seamless. Consumers, especially younger generations, expect connected experiences and more sophisticated means of moving from online channels into the store and back again.

The second theme is the increasing desire for personalization. I remember shopping with my grandmother in Cincinnati when I was a little girl: she would arrive at her favorite department store and the ladies would flutter around her, asking about my grandfather, expressing how big I was getting, and serving us our favorite cookies—all while pulling things off the shelves they knew my grandma would like. Whether it was a department store, drugstore, or the corner beauty shop, she was known everywhere she went. Without a doubt, some of this was my grandmother's uncanny ability to make friends wherever she went. But the key to success in retail was always about knowing your customer. Today, only the most high-end apparel shopping services offer anything close to a personalized experience, and even then, any pre-shopping that occurs online isn't carried through to the retail environment.

While the very concept of "local" has changed over the past decade, we now have more tools at our disposal than ever before to improve upon even our grandmothers' hyperlocal and deeply personalized retail experiences. As an industry, we need to move beyond basic targeting, tracking, and demographic segmentation to drive deeper, permissioned engagement with consumers, where we deliver valuable and *personal* experiences in and out of the store, across every screen.

The following stages describe the ways consumers are making decisions along their path to purchase within the retail environment, as well as the influencers marketers can use to move them through efficiently, addressing the needs of their target audience as they engage with content across screens.

Open to Possibility

Unlike more considered purchase journeys, such as car shopping, habitual journeys are typically triggered by the need to replenish a specific product or set of products. The Open to Possibility moment comes later in the journey, and can slide in prompted by a coupon, an ad, word of mouth, or inspiration at the shelf.

For considered purchases, Open to Possibility is a consumer's current state; it contains her awareness of products and brands that are available, as well as all the past experiences and associations she may have accumulated over time. These can range from reading about new HD televisions in the Technology section of the *New York Times* to seeing your friend's amazing new flat screen television when you go over to his house to watch the latest episode of *Homeland*.

The influencers at this stage are typically recessive: for more considered purchases, such as consumer electronics, 40 percent of consumers are driven by a desire for something newer. But for habitual purchases, such as personal care or groceries, most consumers are driven by a need to replenish their current products. Advertising can still play a role with 12 percent of U.S. consumers influenced by seeing an advertisement on television or online.[2]

Decision to Buy or Change

For habitual purchases, the trigger to buy or change a product happens most frequently when a consumer runs out of an existing product. Considered purchases begin when consumers get the go-ahead from family members or other stakeholders—essentially, permission to make a change and subsequently begin to research a new product. That makes sense considering that they're about to spend a bit more money than they would on a lipstick or bag of chips. The trigger to get the go-ahead happens either when an existing device is old or underperforming or when exposure to newer and flashier products (through advertising or word of mouth) sparks the desire for a more state-of-the-art item.

Evaluating

Habitual consumers spend a bit of time preparing for their shopping trip at this stage; they typically make a list and select the store they will visit, but they generally don't complete extensive research before getting into the retail environment. The bulk of the research consumers do at this stage is focused on where they can get the best deals for the items on their list, but this can be pretty painstaking. Flipping through fliers for deals or coupons, scrolling through e-mails to find promotions for the products on their list, or searching retailer websites for promotions can be a needle-and-haystack exercise. Consumers want personalized offers that dovetail with their shopping list, but this isn't happening as much as they'd like.

In the Evaluating stage, considered shoppers leverage their personal worldview as a "way in" to their decision. This could include a proclivity for more technologically advanced or green products. They'll get a sense of the marketplace—what's available and how much it will cost. Then, consumers home in on specifics, focusing on specs and features and narrowing down their brand consideration set. It's notable that at this stage, consumer enjoyment is at an all-time high; in fact, they enjoy this stage even more than the in-store Shopping stage. This is largely because doing product and brand research is now relatively seamless thanks to the immense amount of information in the digital space. In Chapter 2, we talked about the computer as the Sage; the ability to tap into information, facts, advice, and intelligence around brands and products really comes to the forefront at this stage in the journey. Marketers should capitalize on this by enabling inspiration through digital channels on tablets and computers—experiences that help consumers dream and imagine what's possible—and then enabling them to take self-driven and informative journeys to learn more.

Personalization is also critical. Consumers want to envision how a product will fit into their lives and meet their specific needs, whether it's having a surround sound system built into their television because they host movie nights once a week or finding the thinnest possible mounted screen that won't dominate the living room.

Shopping

Most habitual shoppers still prefer to buy items in store. In the retail environment, their decision making is influenced by deals, packaging, and the more tactile attributes of the product at the shelf, such as scent, product look and feel, and in-store samples. Habitual shoppers will typically complete their list and then enjoy a little browsing and "me time" in-store. This is where consumers find the most enjoyment because they're able to tick off items from their list, while also exploring what other interesting products are out there. This came as a big surprise to us—we always imagined that habitual purchases were pretty cut and dry: *I need new toothpaste and razor blades, and I want to get in and out of the store as quickly as possible.* But instead, consumers actually want to linger and explore—so what can we do to capitalize on the fact that habitual consumers are actually open to the possibility of trying new things once they get into the retail environment?

Again, personalization comes to the forefront. If en route to buying deodorant, I suddenly discover a face mask that helps address some dry skin issues I'm having or find a shower gel on offer that delivers the same benefits as my usual brand, I'll be much more inclined to deviate from my list and try something new. But, as marketers, we're still not delivering this personalization, including providing meaningful and pertinent information at the shelf to facilitate decision making.

By comparison, considered purchasers are much more pragmatic. All of the enjoyment happened when they were doing their research at home. Now consumers know what they want, so they aim to locate their product in store, do just enough browsing and price checking to validate their decision, and then go through a quick and efficient check-out process. Very few considered purchase consumers like to linger in the store for fear they'll be preyed upon by eager salespeople or overwhelmed by too many choices.

How can marketers take the enjoyment of the digital research phase and perpetuate it in store? This is a key moment where we need to start breaking down the barriers between the digital and the real, and we've subsequently identified three key routes in. First, all of the research that consumers do online disappears when they get in store. The sales associate is not privy to any of the research that's been done at home, forcing consumers to rattle off the details of what they're looking for and risk getting sidetracked or upsold. We need to start exploring ways of arming salespeople with the basic data and information gathered online so when consumers get to the store, they aren't starting from scratch.

Second, the exploratory, information-rich digital world that drove so much enjoyment doesn't exist in the retail environment. The need here is for enrichment. How can we use screens in store to engage, inspire, and interest consumers? It could involve something as simple as customizing or configuring devices to support the desire for personalization or watching a television already programmed with the shows you enjoy, which you share seamlessly via a mobile app that collects your viewing habits.

Third, how can we take the friction-free online purchase transaction and replicate it in store? One of the reasons why consumers "showroom"—research online, browse in store, purchase online—is because it is simply easier to buy things in a digital environment. Chances are, our credit card information is already stored, we don't have to wait in line, we can easily select the optimal shipping options and check out in under four minutes.

As marketers, we need to bring this ease and automation to the in-store purchase experience and shift away from what is typically a much more labored, manual process.

Experiencing

In the final stage of the journey, habitual shoppers use their products at home and seek to validate their choice via their own experience with the product, as well as what's fed back to them from others.

Considered shoppers set up their new product and start using it. If it's a consumer electronics item, they may experience some friction if instructions are complicated or absent. Over time, these consumers will also seek validation that they've made a good decision. They are less likely to share or advocate for a retailer or product unless their decision has been validated by others.

Key Takeaways

The retail study flags three key takeaways for multi-screen marketers. The first is to embrace showrooming. While this concept strikes fear in the hearts of many retailers struggling to compete with Amazon, consumers are simply too savvy these days to avoid it. Combat price wars and a "race to the bottom" via value-add services and digital experiences that drive differentiation within the context of each screen. Replicate the ease of digital purchases in store through mobile devices. Make it easy for consumers to see value beyond price with side-by-side comparisons of product features that enable consumers to easily compare and eliminate what doesn't fit. Help them purchase for their families (habitual) or get the go-ahead (considered) with cloud-based list and image-sharing functionality they can pull down from any device. Alongside price and product information, provide reviews, expert opinions, and employee perspectives to deepen enrichment and move beyond function. Take the "showroom" beyond the walls of the store by making both functional information and more emotional experiences accessible on the go—that means mobiles take center stage.

The second takeaway is what we call "minding the gaps." It's important in this day and age not to lose the consumer in the hand-off from the digital to the physical worlds. Capture consumer habits and preferences online through functional tools that offer a clear value for consumers. Then, leverage the data you have about your customers to deliver personal experiences at each step of the journey. If you have loyalty and reward cards, you know what your customers are purchasing. Using these data to make their in-store experiences more personal and more valuable can make a clear difference.

And while it's even more important that customer service and sales associates in store provide inventory assistance, they can be doing more. Technologies such as Skype can help consumers engage sales associates for basic questions before and after making purchases, while relevant experts such as nutritionists, pediatricians, and fitness and tech professionals can offer advice on behalf of your store to provide personalization.

Finally, curate experiences. Pull brand expression into the store with more interactive experiences, and don't make your customers do all the work. Set up areas where they can test and experience products outside of the packaging. Encourage them to interact through in-store touch screens that amplify the product features and benefits. Displays are no longer static, so enable mobile and in-store technology to bring at-the-self personalization, where consumers can pull in accessories or other products that complement one another. Include access to reviews, expert ratings, and in-store recommendations at every point in the process, both on large screens and via mobile technology.

Figures 3.1 and 3.2 summarize the findings of the retail study, and highlight both the biggest influencers along the path to purchase, as well as new opportunities to help ease the way for consumers.

Stage of the Journey	Top Influencers	Top Consumer Needs	Top Screens
Open to Possibility	Family, past experiences, wants vs. needs	Discovery (Enrichment)	TV, Computer, Tablet, Mobile. Feed consumer's curiosity and with enriching lifestyle content around the hottest new tech to drive desire for something new
Decision to Buy or Change	Partner, kids, tech sites, online retailer sites, price comparison sites, consumer opinion sites	Few influencers help consumers get the information or validation they need to "get permission" to make a change	Computer, Tablet. Drive pre-shop anticipation with enriching online experiences around products. Link consumers to consumer opinion and price comparison sites where they can be reassured of value and quality
Evaluating	Consumer opinion sites, brand/product sites, tech sites, online retailer sites, physical retailer site, price comparison site, search, partner	Personalization (underserved) and Enrichment (underserved at "homing in" phase)	Computer, Games Console Mobile and Tablet. Provide enriching and informative digital experiences that allow consumers to get a "feel" for the product from their living room, in the store, or on the go
Shopping	Tech sites, product format, deal sites, promotions and deals, tech/electrical store	Personalization and Information (both undeserved)	Mobile and Tablet, in-store screens (if online shopping, then computer). Make it easy for consumers to explore the tactile aspects of the product via testing areas in the store or rich media and video online. Encourage browsing with personalized suggestions of related products
Experiencing	Friends and family	Personalization and Enrichment	TV, Tablet, Mobile. Solicit feedback from consumers and use it to personalize their shopping experience on future trips

Figure 3.1   The Consumer Decision Journey: Considered Retail Cheat Sheet

Stage of the Journey	Top Influencers	Top Consumer Needs	Top Screens
Open to Possibility	Promotions and deals, in-store samples, product scent, look and touch, product labels	Personalization	Computer, Tablet, Mobile. Drive pre-intention anticipation for something new by helping consumers anticipate what they'll need next week, help them get their list started, get deals and discover new and differentiated products or areas of the store they might want to visit
Decision to Buy or Change	Running out, wanting something new	Personalization	Computer, Tablet, Mobile. Send personalized deals and offers as consumers start running out of their product
Evaluating	Samples, flyers, deal sites, e-mail offers, digital ads	Personalization is top need, but is underserved	Computer and Mobile. Let consumers choose samples to create more "Open to Possibility" moments, while satisfying the consumer desire to understand how a product fits her/him specifically
Shopping	Promos and deals, in-store samples, usual grocery store, product look and format, scent, deal sites, flyers, product labels	Personalization and information are key but are underserved	Mobile in store. Enable personalization through mobile tools that suggest products based on personal preference or point-of-sale screens that help consumer explore tactile elements via curated content (e.g., scan skin cream to discover related products). Encourage discovery with surprise deals and samples she can "unlock" via mobile and in-store navigation tools that make it easy to complete her list
Experiencing	Product performance, partner, friends	Validation	Computer, Tablet, Mobile. Solicit feedback from consumers online and use it to personalize their future shopping trips

Figure 3.2 The Consumer Decision Journey: Habitual Retail Cheat Sheet

THE CONSUMER DECISION JOURNEY: SKIN CARE AND HAIR CARE

One of the most compelling findings from our journey research happened when we set out to discover what motivates women when they shop for skin care and hair care products. Every day, women all over the world experience a continual cycle of dissatisfaction, inspiration, and validation when considering their beauty routines. While 66 percent of grocery buying is habitual,[3] when it comes to beauty products, making a change is an emotionally loaded decision, often involving myriad media channels across devices, plus the opinions and influences of friends, family, and social networks. When you consider that three in five women change skin care products at least once every three months,[4] that's a lot of angst!

What we find is that women experience a slow and steady build-up of dissatisfaction before making a change in their hair care or skin care routine. Once they decide to change products, they find themselves on a quest for definitive and trustworthy advice. Then, they face their worst nightmare: The Dreaded Shelf. The Consumer Decision Journey for Retail, which we were inspired to conduct on the back of our findings from this study, flags up a range of solutions that marketers can employ to counteract this consumer frustration at the shelf (refer to previous section of this chapter).

Throughout this journey, the pendulum swings from dissatisfaction to inspiration to validation, and then back to dissatisfaction again. But what forces cause women to consider a change? And how are they validating their decision? Let's move through the stages of the decision journey, exploring, by way of example, what happens when a woman decides she wants a new bottle of shampoo.

Open to Possibility

Once upon a time, our shampoo seeker wasn't even aware that she wanted to make a change. But everyday life brings her into contact with hints that her hair is not perfect; health and beauty sites, magazines, celebrities, and TV ads play a part, but so does seeing friends on social networks or in person. Issues with her hair, often prompted by looking enviously at other women's "better" hair, build up. The elicited emotions are almost all negative— words like "struggle," "angry," "clueless," and "envy" come up frequently with consumers in our in-depth interviews.

And this leads us to one of the biggest influencers at this stage: mom. Time and again, the women we spoke to mention their mother as a key trigger for dissatisfaction. And I can attest that a single word from my mom about looking tired, run-down, or "needing a haircut" will send me off to my nearest drugstore in search of a sexy new hair care or skin care product to demonstrate to my mother that I really do know how to take of myself (at the ripe old age of 30-something, no less).

This more passive stage is characterized by the slow build-up of dissatisfaction with her hair care or skin care regimen. The tipping point is when the consumer decides she needs to find a better product solution.

Decision to Buy or Change

At this second stage in her journey, our shampoo seeker is tuned in to all the influences around her. She is more aware of relevant product advertising across all media, particularly if it's in the right context, such as beauty sites, blogs, and magazines. While the TV, computers, and mobile phones all play roles here, television has a more diffuse influence than either the mobile or the computer. The odds are slim that a woman will see a television ad for shampoo that addresses her specific need at the right moment, unless she watches five hours of television a day. So while television plays an important role for early branding, computers, tablets, and mobile phones can offer more personalization.

Just feeling as though she's taking control of her problem can cause a shift to a more positive mind-set. She feels "positive," "upbeat," and "open" as she seeks a solution. At the Decision to Buy or Change stage, she is actively seeking a way to fix her problem and feel better about her hair. She is looking for trusted advice—and the more definitive the advice she receives, the easier the rest of the buying process becomes. This is a critical phase for marketers to get into her consideration set by both inspiring her and providing her with relevant product information.

Evaluating

Now, our shampoo seeker has admitted that she's dissatisfied with her hair, and she's found enough evidence to prove she can do something about it. She hasn't yet had that final push into taking action, however, as there hasn't been the definitive piece of advice or reassurance to get her going. It doesn't take much to tip the balance by now, though she tends to be more passive here—sitting back and waiting for the final piece of the puzzle to fall into place.

She's still in a positive mood, but there's enough doubt in her mind to hold her back from making a purchase. She doesn't have quite enough confidence to act yet. Friends and her hairdresser play critical roles at this stage. Coupons start to make an appearance, as well as samples—both limit the amount of risk she takes on and may move her to take action and buy a new hair care product.

A final push leads her to decide on a product. Occasionally, the push is specific enough to speed her through to purchase. More typically, she has an idea of what she wants, but is trying to build commitment by either increasing confidence (through reviews, recommendations, and information) or reducing risk (using samples, coupons or discounts). She rarely does both at the same time, however, and uses both her laptop and mobile phone to access the information she needs.

Any lack of a definitive answer, or not enough information from the brands she's looking into, can push her back into negative emotions—feeling "clueless" and "angry"—and a sense of "struggle" pervades as she deals with an abundance of choice in hair care products.

Shopping

When she moves into the retail environment, unless she's had the specific and final piece of advice she was seeking, the consumer has to employ whatever tactics she can to narrow down her choice. She is on her own once she gets to the store—her perception is that people and media channels are nearly absent. Filtering mechanisms she uses to help herself can include coupons and deals, brand, or keywords such as "frizzy," "dry," or "volume."

Her actions at this stage depend on how informed and reassured she is when she enters the store. If she's fixed on a brand, then this stage is approached with optimism. If she hasn't yet been through the filtering process and landed on what she wants, she's cautious, with feelings of "cluelessness" and "struggle" amplified by a lack of time and evidence with which to make a decision.

After our shampoo seeker has reduced the consideration set to a few brands, she simply has to make her final choice. The brand is generally the only source of information used at this point. In the absence of any other cues, the decision can often come down to something as simple as which bottle contains the nicest scent.

Once again, this experience is influenced by how well armed she has been with evidence and advice before reaching the store. She's done the hard work of winnowing down the full wall of bottles, so negative feelings are not quite as pronounced as before. But if she had an easy way of analyzing and comparing the specific information about each hair care product, she'd have even more confidence in her decision, allowing her to make an informed choice quickly.

Experiencing

Our consumer may have her shampoo in hand, but it's not over yet. This first key usage stage can be completed quickly; often women can be happy with the product based on a single use, with the mirror giving immediate feedback on the success or failure of the product. A more involved "problem" may require repeat usage, however.

Assuming the product works, the feelings are all positive: we hear consumers continually say they feel "empowered," "happy," "successful," and even "relief" if previous experiences have been poor. If the product fails to meet her needs, then emotions are negative, often focused on the waste of money and the need to repeat what has already been a difficult decision-making process.

Despite the validation of the mirror, what others think does matter. If you've ever found yourself checking reviews after making a purchase, a somewhat counterintuitive practice, you were likely seeking validation. Humans are social to the core, and the wisdom of crowds is nearly always important to us. The most important validation comes from her inner circle: her husband, daughter, and friends. The more feedback she has from this group, and the more she restricts herself to this group, the longer her period of satisfaction with the product lasts. A positive comment from her hairdresser can also help. But eventually, she'll seek more validation through sources such as magazines, celebrity sites, and TV ads and shows. Ironically, she's now exposing herself to the same sources that triggered dissatisfaction in the first place, starting the entire process again.

The final stage of external validation can move from reassurance, satisfaction, and happiness to uncertainty if any doubt starts to creep in. Uncertainty tends to be triggered only when validation is sought from sources outside of her inner circle and when she doesn't get the information or support she needs to feel good about her product choice.

Key Takeaways

How can marketers inspire confidence when women are making decisions about which beauty products to buy? We'll serve up some detailed solutions when we take you through the case study at the end of this chapter. But at a high level, brands that provide relevant information through trusted sources that help women feel good about the product they buy can lead to long-term brand loyalty.

There are five key takeaways marketers should keep in mind. The first is to enable subtle encounters that seed ideas. The BermanBraun and Microsoft–created Glo.com's rich magazine-like digital experiences enable women to immerse themselves in an aspirational contextual environment. And the tablet itself is a fantastic screen to enable these encounters, as women using tablets tend to be in a more exploratory state of mind.

Second, organize digital content that brings in both relevant health and beauty information. Consider creating a Care Hub, curating relevant skin care, hair care, and beauty information.

Third, connect women with others at crucial decision-making junctures. Skype and similar services can enable conversation in a personal, one-on-one environment with friends, family, or experts and influencers.

Fourth, show digital content via mobile technologies that reinforce messaging at the shelf to improve spend consideration. That can include expert and consumer reviews or even information she can easily customize, such as suggestions for curly hair.

And finally, don't forget to validate her decision. Provide access to videos created by beauty and health experts; focus on healthy skin techniques and solutions that augment her skin care solutions and reinforce her choice.

Figure 3.3 summarizes the key influencers along the beauty path to purchase and highlights opportunities for marketers to meet the needs of beauty shoppers.

Stage of the Journey	Top Influencers	Top Consumer Needs	Top Screens
Open to Possibility	Mom, partner, friends, health and beauty sites, consumer opinion sites, samples/trials, tv/mag ads	Personalization is top need but few media influencers have strong impact	TV, Tablet. Become a trusted source to provide the information she needs/experiences that will guide her toward your brand (e.g., provide access to beauty videos by experts, let her enter her skin concerns and provide content around solutions)
Decision to Buy or Change	Health and beauty sites, samples/trials, brand sites, workplace, mom, partner, consumer opinion sites	Personalization and Information are top needs but few influencers meet these needs	Computer, Tablet. Let her choose samples/trial versions to be delivered to her home so she can test out the products before she gets in the store
Evaluating	Deal and coupon sites, samples/trials, consumer opinion sites, healthcare professional, beauty specialists	Information and Enrichment. Expert opinions are very impactful, but fewer consumers have access	Computer, Tablet, Games Console, Mobile. Organize digital content on a "care hub"—provide access to videos by experts, let her enter her skin concerns and provide content and reviews about product solutions
Shopping	Samples/trials, health and beauty sites	No influencers meet Enrichment, Comprehension, or Confidence (which creates uncertainty at the shelf)	Mobile. Show digital content via mobile that reinforces messaging at the shelf to improve spend consideration and reinforce confidence
Experiencing	Samples/trials/coupons, friends, partner, health and beauty sites, brand sites, deal/coupon sites, store, partner	Few influencers meet the top needs of Personalization, Confidence and Enrichment	Computer, Tablet, Mobile. Create easy sharing tools through social channels

Figure 3.3   The Consumer Decision Journey: Beauty Cheat Sheet

The Consumer Decision Journey: Food and Beverage

My friend Kate is a poet and a mom in Pennsylvania facing all the challenges and joys of single parenthood—including what to feed her family on a day-to-day basis. In any typical day, Kate's five-year-old daughter refuses to eat any food item beyond white rice and yogurt, while going after anything containing sugar with stunning determination. Meanwhile, Kate's dad, who lives nearby and often babysits, has a weakness for salty snacks, but his doctor says he needs to lose weight. Kate herself is less picky, but like 78 percent of moms,[5] she prefers to find snacks that she would enjoy eating alongside her children.

In short, Kate wants to buy snacks that her family enjoys, but she also wants them to be reasonably healthy. When it comes to buying food, Kate is in a constant state of consideration, but making a decision that meets the needs of her entire family is becoming more difficult as their needs and tastes diverge.

Despite an overwhelming number of advertising messages, there aren't many resources that actually help. When Kate enters the grocery store, it's Mom versus The Shelf . . . and her daughter is on The Shelf's side. Kate's dilemma is not uncommon. This is how moms like her travel through the decision journey for food and beverages. It's important to note that we conducted this research with only moms, so while we don't mean to leave dads out of the equation, we're using moms as the example here. One could likely substitute "parents" throughout, especially if dad takes on the weekly grocery shopping.

Open to Possibility

In this first decision phase, parents like Kate openly consider the myriad food and beverage options for their families. In fact, Kate is almost always open to new suggestions, and there are plenty of sources of influence: 53 percent of moms said they would like a way to keep track of a rolling list of inspiration and ideas for family snacks.[6] Like other moms, Kate is most attuned to those close to her—her daughter, her dad, her sister—but her wider circle can be almost as influential. Other moms whom she intersects with at the playground or school drop-off can tune her into new snack options or make her question some of her current choices.

Media is another source of influence, from online or offline advertising to print or web-based articles covering topics like nutrition, healthy food options, and recipes for the family. Coupons and deals can also act as a shortcut to consideration. Reduce risk here, and she's likely to narrow her consideration set quickly and move right into the store. Says one mom we interviewed, "I'll look to see what's on sale and stock up if it's something I like. But I stay with brands, and I buy what I want and won't just buy because it's on sale."

One of the perennial truths about many moms is that they are always caught up in the risk of buying something that their family won't eat—which is not only a waste of money, but makes them feel both guilty and annoyed that they aren't attuned to their family's tastes.

Decision to Buy or Change

As Kate begins to commit to changing what she buys or trying something new, her emotions are tied up with the need to be a good mom. Doing so requires balancing multiple needs and demands, while also trying to avoid conflict; 95 percent of moms said they place the most importance on their family's needs with a dual focus on what needs to be replenished.[7]

The second thing moms in our study do when they hit the Decision to Change stage is write out their shopping list. Once again, there are few sources of inspiration or influence as she's making her list, although her kids and partner may weigh in with suggestions—albeit of varying degrees of helpfulness. Kate is trying to balance the input she gets with her knowledge of the items that actually need to be replaced. With a large and continually updated set of options, few tools currently exist to help her filter them down. Lists are compiled quickly and often in shorthand: bread, milk, cereal, toothpaste, and fruit/veg.

This is where emotions start coming into sharper focus. The pressures of balancing demands, avoiding conflict, and above all being a good mom become very important. She's left on her own to balance the needs of nutrition, kids' demands, taste, and variety, with nothing in place to help her land on the best decisions; given this, it isn't surprising that 75 percent of moms said they would like to have a tool to help them organize deals in the list-making stage.[8] The sought-after tool isn't just an app that helps her make a digital list that she can take in store, but also folds in offers, deals, nutrition information, recipe ideas—in other words, helps her compile a list that enables her to address the wide-ranging and complex needs that drive her food purchase decisions.

The third step in the Decision to Buy or Change stage involves getting specific product details around ingredients, nutritional value, benefits, taste, quantity, and price. After Kate makes her list, she wants to get enough detail to help her make a decision that balances out her needs around being a good mom—finding snacks that are low in sugar, have added vitamins, or are free of high fructose corn syrup—while not neglecting the realities of what her kids will actually eat. Ultimately, moms like Kate are seeking balance and variety: good nutrition that tastes great so kids stay healthy and happy, combined with variety to keep her children from getting bored. When you think about it, this is a reasonably tall order—and something that moms need to weigh out week after week, month after month. We need to think about what we can do as marketers to give her the information and facts she needs to make this decision as streamlined and easy as possible.

Evaluating

At the Evaluating stage, which is the classic research phase in the decision journey, there are three steps consumers experience before moving to the actual purchase. The first is Taking Inventory. The snacking purchase journey becomes more active at this point, usually prompted by a weekly shopping trip. In this phase, moms usually have categories of snacks that they are seeking to fill, such as cookies, crackers, and potato chips. Working out what has run out guides her toward the new items she's been toying with buying—if she needs to stock up on salty snacks, then she's more likely to think about all the other options in this category. There are few sources that either help or influence her as she moves through this process, although her family is always in the background offering "helpful" suggestions.

The emotions from the Decision to Buy or Change stage and desire to be a good mom are still in play, but at this point, emotions take a bit of a back seat. Since this phase is really research focused, the emphasis is on fact finding. She's seeking balance and variety still. One of the few ways of filtering the consideration set is to seek deals, coupons, and offers. Not only does this help to narrow her choices, it minimizes the risks of making a "wrong" decision. At this stage, the research focus is less on ingredients, nutritional information, and product benefits as she becomes much more attuned to finding the brand that offers the benefits she seeks at the best price. Online searches, looking for e-mail deals, and sifting through print publications, such as circulars or local papers, comes to the fore.

With so many new products being launched, there are often trial offers available, making the decision a little easier. Kate remains aware of the pressures of getting the right product that her family will eat and is anticipating the stressful shopping trip, so emotions may run high. Coupons can lower the risk of mom making a mistake and buying something the family doesn't like. One mom said, "I'll look at coupons online, but only for things I will use." Food websites are also influential here as a final check; 45 percent of moms said they want more ways to connect health-related information to recipes and snack ideas.[9]

Shopping

As Kate moves into the store, her shopping list rarely specifies brands or goes into product details—BBQ Flavored Chex Mix, low sodium variant. Instead, the focus is on the broader category of item: fruit snack, rice cakes, potato chips, ice cream. As a result, this is a stage of filtering and cost-benefit analysis squeezed into a very small amount of time, often conjuring up feelings of "Mom versus The Shelf." Not only does Kate have to tackle the shelf alone—the bewildering mix of products, finding the brand and variant she seeks and looking for promotions or deals—she also has to keep her daughter occupied at the same time (who surreptitiously may just drop cookies into the shopping cart).

What she really needs right now are solutions to make all of these at-the-shelf decisions easier and help her land on the optimal brand, product, and price/deal/promotion that meets her full suite of needs. There are many opportunities for technology to sort through the confusion of the in-store stage; 55 percent of moms said they would like a phone app that helps them get recommendations and deals in store; and 26 percent are currently using their smart phones to get food- and snack-related information.[10]

Experiencing

Finally, at the Experiencing stage of the decision journey, Kate has come home with her weekly supplies and new snacks in hand and is ready to open her cupboard to the family. As you might imagine, she feels a welcome sense of relief. The payoff she gets when she sees her family enjoying the snacks cannot be underestimated. She pays close attention to her successes, feeding this back into her consideration process and sharing these with friends and extended family. This isn't just a charitable act; it allows her to show off that she's in-the-know; 40 percent of moms said friends and family ask for their advice on snack-related purchases—and 33 percent will often write reviews of items they've recently purchased.[11] Says one mom, "There were these granola bars a friend had that my kids loved, but I couldn't find them anywhere! I went to store after store. I even posted on Facebook to see if my friends knew where to get them."

Getting validation from other mothers—including her own—gives her the confidence that she's not only made the right decision, but that she's a good mom.

Key Takeaways

Understanding how consumers navigate these five stages of the decision journey and identifying how the digital world wraps around each stage are both crucial to mastering marketing in the digital era. There are three critical insights to keep top of mind:

First, you can use screens to help lower her risk. Samples can give her a reason to try new products—but they should be personalized when possible. Sending her a sample for pretzels when her children eat gluten-free will be a wasted effort. Deliver e-mail and mobile offers with tips on how snacks feature into her family's day to inspire her. Online content that provides her with inspiration to see what works and doesn't work for other moms like her has a big influence.

Second, arm her with information via mobile to battle "The Shelf." The earlier in the journey you can drive a decision, the lower the risk of causing conflict with her kids. Focus on affirming the right choice and reducing risk of the wrong choice (coupons, samples). Facilitate shopping lists on e-mail and via mobile to help her customize and improve her experience when she's in the store. Mobile enables a great way to stay organized, search for more information on the go, find recipes, and keep her ideas in one place.

Finally, encourage sharing. Moms need validation and inspiration. Encourage her to share her experiences through social and lifestyle channels with multiple resources to get feedback and tell her stories. You can also put her in touch with experts—pediatricians, nutritionists, chefs—who will provide additional validation for her decisions. Moms are always plagued with the concern that they could do better, and whatever we can do as marketers to alleviate their worries and give them confidence will drive loyalty and advocacy around a brand.

The Consumer Journey: Snacks Cheat Sheet (Figure 3.4) summarizes our research, as well as areas of opportunity for marketers.

THE CONSUMER DECISION JOURNEY: AUTO BUYERS

Cars are a major purchase, and one might assume that for many people, selecting and purchasing a new car is a very rational decision. But we often underplay the emotional factors that persist throughout the decision journey. Cars evoke a sense of freedom . . . and even first love. In established markets, people start out with preconceived ideas and brand preferences that are difficult to

Stage of the Journey	Top Influencers	Top Consumer Needs	Top Screens
Open to Possibility	Kids, partner	Personalization	TV, Tablet. She is constantly looking for ideas; inspire her confidence with compelling content around new snacks that may work for her family's needs
Decision to Buy or Change	Partner, kids, grocery stores, samples/trials, health sites, circulars	Personalization— no influencers help her envision how the product would work for her and her family	Computer, Tablet, Mobile. Samples give her a great reason to try new products. Embed tips in e-mail and give her access to online coupon/trial offers
Evaluating	Partner, kids, sample/ trials, food sites, e-mails (friends), grocery shops, events, circulars, e-mail (deals/offers)	Visualization and projection are key but few influencers serve those needs	Computer, Tablet, Mobile. Spend consideration is highest when she's taking inventory, so key to reach her at this point
Shopping	Kids, partner, samples/trials, food sites, events, grocery shops, shopping sites	No sources to organize Information, which can make shopping overwhelming	Mobile. Arm her with information to battle the shelf—facilitate shopping lists on e-mail or mobile that help her keep organized, search for info on the go and keep ideas in one place
Experiencing	Kids, partner, samples, food sites, grocery shops, e-mail (friends)	Confidence (validation) is key but unmet by media influencers	Computer, tablet, mobile. Encourage her to share her experiences with other moms through social and lifestyle channels

Figure 3.4 The Consumer Decision Journey: Snacks Cheat Sheet

change. These can include nostalgia around what our dads drove (Chevy Chevettes!) or the first car we owned in high school. But consumers still feel pressure to work out what they want and how they approach the buying process.

Our auto-buyers research reveals five key stages on the path to purchase. The first three stages build clarity, and the last two build confidence. What the consumer decision journey for autos demonstrates is that marketers no longer have a captive audience that can be reached through a few great television and print ads. As a result, it's difficult to know and understand where you should invest marketing dollars along the decision journey for optimal impact.

Both consumers and marketers find themselves in a challenging new environment, where too many choices and complexity can often obfuscate the right solution or purchase decision at any given time. But knowing how to harness digital channels can help start to close that divide, reaching and inspiring consumers at the right place and time, with the right content, which can help clarify choices and enable easier decision making.

Open to Possibility

Cars are everywhere, and they've influenced us consciously or unconsciously from the time we were children. From what our parents drove, to the advertising campaigns we see on television, every encounter we have with cars shapes our perception. Some consumers, especially in developed markets, such as the United States and the U.K., have established solid brand preferences over the course of their lives, which help them move through their auto-buying journey faster and with more certainty. Other individuals may approach car buying in a more open way. This openness, however, can often prolong the decision-making process, requiring people to start from scratch as they embark on their journey.

Decision to Buy or Change

Over time, a consumer's new car becomes his current car. Some purchases are driven by the age of the car, while for others, the motivation to purchase a new car is linked to a life-change: the birth of a child, a new job in a new city, or the freedom of becoming an empty nester. Very occasionally the motivation may be the strong desire for a specific car—a desire that can be driven purely through advertising.

Consumers are usually motivated to make a change because of personal circumstances. But some consumers admit they simply buy a new car simply because they want one. The fabled midlife crisis car neatly fits into this mind-set.

Evaluating

The Evaluating stage is where consumers are just beginning to roll up their sleeves and start their research. There are generally four steps that the consumer has to work through: confirming if he or she is going to buy a new car, working out what he or she wants from a new car, determining the key information sources to make the decision, and establishing a sense of the brands or models that are out there. Those with solid brand preferences or past experience get through this stage quickly and easily, but most consumers have trouble with some, or all, of these steps. In some cases, it may be difficult for the consumer to work out how to get the information needed to move through each decision phase. What helps many consumers here, however, is taking a lifestyle approach: top 10 family cars or best fuel-efficient car lists give consumers a "way in" to their research.

Shopping

The Shopping stage happens in a unique manner for car buying. Most of the eliminate-and-compare activity that consumers naturally exhibit when researching purchases happens online, well before people make it to the dealership. Three phases make up this decision stage for auto buyers: The Terrain, The Car, and The Deal.

In The Terrain phase, consumers commit to buying a new car. Their consideration set is based on experience, trusted recommendations, advertising, and the light research they did in the Evaluating stage. Some makes and models will not be the right fit, and consumers will eliminate these quickly. After a bit more light exploration, their list of options gets reduced.

At this point, the real work begins: a compare-and-contrast task based on more detailed specs, reviews, seeing the vehicle in person, and—for a few—an early test drive. Consumers need tools online that help them eliminate what doesn't fit and then compare what's left. As you might imagine, personalization and information are both critical at this stage so consumers can get the information they need to make the best choices for their needs. As consumers begin the heavy job of eliminating and comparing options, websites on laptops and tablets provide a single location for reviews, professional ratings, and compelling video, bringing to life a consumer's consideration set.

The second phase is called The Car. Now, consumers are focused on "the one." They've narrowed the choice down to a car, including specifications and options. For some, The Car phase is all about planning negotiation tactics and knowing where to compromise. Others are determined to hunt down the one ideal car at exactly the right price. The easy integration of auto with money content makes it easy for consumers to feel confident before entering negotiations with the dealerships. Local dealership listings via mobile apps enable consumers to leave a dealership they don't like and easily find one nearby that they do.

In the final phase, The Deal, the consumer wants to go to the dealer to buy a specific car, armed with all the facts that he or she needs to get the best price. He or she will want to meet his or her objective—and then get out as fast as possible.

Experiencing

The final stage of the consumer decision journey is focused on the car, how it performs and how others react to it. More than ever, consumers personalize their vehicles through technology, and often discover unexpected features that can drive their advocacy, such as integration with their smartphones via apps and other technologies. This is where consumers not only determine their personal satisfaction with the vehicle, but also seek out external post-purchase validation through reviews, friends, family, and even media. Consumers who sync up their car to their mobile phones are 36 percent more likely to advocate for the brand,[12] so marketers should be highly motivated to educate consumers on how to fully take advantage of their new connected car.

Key Takeaways

For auto dealers and manufacturers, there is one universal lesson to keep in mind. It is critical to understand the emotional and functional needs of consumers at each stage in the journey in order to inform creative content. Before models and specs, you should leverage aggregated lifestyle content such as "Top Ten Family Cars" or "Best City Vehicles" to help consumers establish their unique needs.

Second, and specifically for manufacturers, encourage more consistent dealership involvement in your tier 2 and 3 advertising—create location-aware mobile messages that get consumers into the dealership.

Third, bring the test drive experience to life before the dealership visit through rich media, video, and interactive games: 47 percent of U.S. consumers would like online virtual test drives as well as 360° interior views of the cars they want to drive so that they get a real feel for the cars in their consideration set.[13]

Fourth, deliver a seamless connection between auto decision making and finance on laptops and tablets. Find ways to show different scenarios so consumers have a curated and personalized set of options.

Fifth, help consumers avoid stalling in one stage by providing and storing a combination of authoritative content, expert

Stage of the Journey	Top Influencers	Top Consumer Needs	Top Screens
Open to Possibility	The car your parents drove, cars you've owned, cars on your street, ads and movies	Discovery and excitement (enrichment) ignite desire for something new (aggregated lifestyle content is helpful here, e.g., "Top Ten Family Cars")	TV, tablet, mobile, console. Understand the emotional or functional needs of consumers and provide aggregated lifestyle content
Decision to Buy or Change	Problems with your current car, a life event e.g., a child, a desire for change	Consumers need to be motivated to pull the trigger—brands should aim to be top of mind at this moment	TV, Tablet, Mobile. Encourage dealership involvement—create location-aware mobile messages that get consumers into the dealership
Evaluating	Partner, car review sites, independent car valuation sites, travel/cars in the street	Information is key; switchbacks caused by lack of clarity around car choices as well as financial issues	Computer, Tablet, Mobile, Games Console (opportunity: bring test drive experience to life through rich media, video, interactive games)
Shopping	Partner, car review sites, car comparison sites, car valuation sites, search, travel/cars in street, manufacturer sites, dealer sites	Information and confidence are key; lack of either can cause switchbacks.	Mobile (apps), Tablet. Help consumers avoid switchbacks by providing and storing authoritative content, expert reviews, consumer opinions, and local dealer information across devices
Experiencing	Partner, manufacturer sites, dealer sites, car review sites, travel/cars in street	Validation is key but not all consumers who are validated become brand advocates—need to link both activities more closely	Computer, Tablet, Mobile, TV. Make advocacy easy by helping consumers validate their decision through rich post-purchase campaigns that enable consumers to get mobile alerts, store important information and join like-minded communities for brand advocacy

Figure 3.5 The Consumer Decision Journey: Auto-Buyers Cheat Sheet

reviews, consumer opinions, and local dealer information across multiple devices: 44 percent of U.S. consumers are willing to share their preferences in order to have dealers reach out to them with specific offers.[14]

And finally, make advocacy easy; help consumers validate their decision through rich post-purchase campaigns that enable consumers to get mobile service alerts, store important information, and join like-minded communities where they can become brand advocates.

You can view the stages and sub-phases of the Auto-Buyers Journey in Figure 3.5, as well as the top influencers and key areas of opportunity for marketers.

THE CONSUMER DECISION JOURNEY: FINANCIAL SERVICES

When we set out to conduct the journey study for financial services, we realized we had a unique challenge. How could we get a clear-eyed view of consumer needs across a category that ran the gamut of low involvement purchases, such as auto insurance, all the way up to retirement and investing? Ivy Esquero, an insights manager on our team, came up with an inspired idea. Rather than go deep on one subcategory, we would look at consumer goals across the category and then align those goals with financial services products.

The path to financial decision making is complex for consumers; they are often overwhelmed in the early stages and frequently get stuck with plans and products that don't work for them. Rather than making quick changes, however, many consumers feel a sense of inertia; they know they're not doing enough, but they don't feel sufficiently confident to make a change when needed. As a result, they frequently take an overly passive approach to managing their finances. While consumers allocate 40 percent of their money to achieve financial goals, 60 percent of them worry about achieving these goals.[15] If our worries were dollars, we'd be able to retire tomorrow. Consumers need help juggling financial priorities. Providing tools and ideas to help them manage their entire financial life will help dispel some of the worry and give consumers more confidence in their decision making as they build deeper relationships with their providers.

Open to Possibility (Passive)

Consumers' experiences often set the stage for how they approach a financial goal. Lessons learned from parents and other influencers, earlier experiences, and their own personalities can define how actively or passively they approach their goal: 70 percent of consumers agree that it is more important than ever to have savings,[16] yet only 40 percent are truly confident that they are doing all they can.[17] Saving for the future, including for retirement funds, paying off debt, building emergency and college funds, are all top of mind in the passive Open to Possibility stage.

The biggest need at this stage is to visualize what financial success looks like. Videos and articles centered on real people can help connect on a personal level and encourage consumers to make a plan.

Decision to Buy or Change (Passive)

If a consumer starts his journey from an earlier life stage, or doesn't feel empowered with enough information, he will make a passive decision to set a plan. For example, using the same checking account that was established when he or she was in high school into adulthood. These products or plans are frequently those that are the easiest to obtain, requiring little to no research and virtually no active shopping. Products are often recommended by a strong influencer like a parent or are extended from the portfolio of products already owned (e.g., from current bank or institution).

Only 28 percent of consumers say they have a dollar amount in mind when setting a financial goal,[18] so providing benchmarks or examples of what consumers can achieve will go a long way toward helping them see what they need to do for their own situation. Few consumers are having their personalization needs met at this stage: they need a better understanding of what their goal should be and how they can meet that goal within their current lifestyle. Digital tools and content can be effectively deployed to help them visualize success.

This stage is still passive; consumers need light research and access to simple product comparisons. Links to easy comparisons of rates and benefits can help reassure and provide (not too much) information. Use easy messaging in advertising or connect to advertorials and stories explaining basic terms.

Experiencing (Passive)

This is the "set it and forget it" stage. Consumers know very little about their financial plans and often let them run in the background. There is a vague sense that they need to do more, but inertia and a feeling that a change will be more trouble than it's worth can contribute to even more inertia.

Here, consumers need a jolt that can move them to a more active stage. Many times, this is an artifact of personal behavior; a consumer may suffer from a poor credit score that doesn't enable him to buy a house, for example. This jolt can motivate consumers to start making more active changes. But marketers can also play a role here: 85 percent of consumers feel motivated when their goals are clear, as opposed to 75 percent who have more amorphous targets,[19] so even just helping consumers clarify their goals can be a step in the right direction.

Decision to Buy or Change (Active)

When the "Decision to Buy or Change" becomes more active, it's almost always because consumers experience a life change or an unexpected turn in circumstances that makes them realize that the passive approach is not working. As one consumer told us, "My husband lost his job for a period of time, and we needed to rebuild an emergency cushion."

Here, consumers are determined to start in a better place. Access to content such as "Top Banks" or "Top Accounts for College Savings" can set a more organized approach to evaluating options and help set the stage so consumers feel empowered in their decision. Advertorial content on accounts and feature rankings through news and finance apps can be a big help. Messaging in ads that hits at specific ways a consumer can achieve a goal are often effective.

Evaluating (Active)

In this stage, consumers are actively evaluating the right approach, the right companies, and the right products. They need access to varied sources of information; investigation and personalization are their biggest needs. *How will this product work for me, given my goals and current circumstances?* Personal validation through those closest to them can help tip consumers toward specific products and brands. Communication channels can connect to those closest to them in the crucial Evaluation stage.

Shopping (Active)

In the Shopping stage, the consumer is armed with facts and is actively choosing specific plans, products, and brands. Deep product information and understanding of their full financial picture are critical at this point. Articles and content that dives deeply into more sophisticated products with a personalization element is useful here. Videos and access to experts can also help consumers feel empowered in their choices. Search can connect consumers to helpful sources, as long as they are relevant and lead to personalized content.

Once consumers get their plan in place, they tend to feel hopeful. "I will feel like I can weather most of life's storms," says one U.S. consumer.

Experiencing (Active)

In the final active stage, the goal is within reach, and consumers feel good about their choices. However, they are looking for constant reassurance that they are doing well—they made the right choice and it's paying off. They need continuous feedback from brands, personal contacts, and media that they are on the right track.

It's important to stay on the consumers' radar through brand messaging that provides a personal connection. Articles and advertorials featuring expert opinion or testimonials from "people like me" demonstrating how specific brands and products help consumers achieve and maintain their goals can provide external validation and sanction decisions.

Second, consumers need to build more effective relationships with their financial services providers. While 66 percent of consumers say that it's important to understand the value they get from companies using their data, only 31 percent say they are satisfied. Marketers have to be more transparent about the value exchange they offer and enable consumers to feel in control of their information. When consumers feel satisfied that they are getting something tangible back from sharing their data, they feel empowered.[20] Of those satisfied that they see value in exchanging information, 41 percent say they are doing everything they need (are on the right path) versus only 29 percent of those who don't see the benefit of the exchange. On a basic level, consumers believe that sharing their data should facilitate more personalized, relevant plans, offers, and products.

Key Takeaways

There are three key takeaways for financial service marketers. The first is to provide clarity around financial goals that will build consumer confidence. Guide consumers with personalized signposts showing them how they are doing and how their day-to-day decisions can fit with longer-term priorities. Give context to longer-term goals by juxtaposing them with shorter-term goals, which are easier for consumers to visualize. Providing a view on how different decisions can lead to different outcomes can be incredibly helpful here. Digital tools that allow them to customize different scenarios are effective. Don't forget to give consumers examples to help them envision success with their goal: personal stories can help connect consumers to others who share their circumstances and give them ideas on where to start or where they need to be.

Second, provide consumers with a sense of control over their plan and their information in order to battle inertia. Bad experiences can trigger negativity and feelings of helplessness. You should provide some perspective through balanced reporting and information sharing. Bring in third-party sources or link to experts that consumers trust to give them a sense of the big picture. But be transparent about the value exchange—don't assume consumers know what you can and can't do with their information. Communicate simpler terms of service; give information up front about what data is being kept, what is being used, and how it helps deliver better products and services to consumers.

Finally, connect back with consumers at the right moments to reassure and build trust. Don't let consumers build up anxiety over how you are helping them—out of sight is definitely not out of mind. Consumers need reminders of what you have done for them lately. Reward consumers for loyalty, but only if you've established a relationship first. Providing specialized services such as alerts to better products and rates are welcome. Benchmarks that allow them to see how products stack up can be even better. Advisors have a unique opportunity to connect—not just on long-term goals. They provide a lot of influence, but sometimes this influence is too diffuse or not centered on consumer needs or goals. Redirect the conversation to fulfill personalization for maximum impact. But remember to start slowly with new customers—fewer are willing to share deep information, but most will open up over time as you build trust.

Figure 3.6 provides an easy summary of the Financial Services research, including top influencers and key opportunities for marketers.

If you've made it through every journey, you can see that while each vertical is unique, some similar threads come to the forefront, including the need for consumers to understand how products or services fit their lives. Now, we're going to take a look at a case study that brings many of the principles of the journey framework to life, including the need for personalized content that facilitates decision making, as well as validation from others: *Does this product fit my life? Can I imagine myself using it? Do others like it, too?* What's most compelling about the Pretty in My Pocket case study, in fact, is that simply fulfilling a customer need where it's not being served can open up an entirely new business model.

Stage of the Journey	Top Influencers	Top Consumer Needs	Top Screens
Open to Possibility	Parents, past experiences, personality (i.e., risk-averse vs. aggressive)	Consumers need a sense of security and belonging in order to begin a more active journey	Television, Tablet enables content early in the journey
Passive—Decision to Buy or Change	Long term: Financial advisors, spouse, work, financial news sites, account information Mid and Short term: Spouse, search, work, account information, bank and financial news sites	Few needs are served for consumers who don't have advisors. Visualizing success and gaining confidence through investigation are key needs	Computer provides tools and information; Tablet and Mobile enables quick tools on-the-go
Active—Evaluating, Shopping and Experiencing	Long term: Financial advisors, spouse, work, financial news sites, statements (online and offline), e-mail, search, bank sites and media Mid and Short term: spouse, search, work, account info, bank sites and financial news sites	Long term: While spouse, advisor, full-service brokerage sites and financial TV programs are relatively stronger than other influencers in serving Projection and Confidence, when you look at all the top influencers, they are not serving the top two needs well. On average, delivery for projection is 33% and confidence is 25% Mid and Short term: Only one's partner helps fulfill confidence and comprehension well	TV can fulfill expertise via financial news shows. Computer content provides deeper investigation tools, while mobile apps and tools are becoming essential for ongoing management

Figure 3.6 The Consumer Decision Journey: Financial Services Cheat Sheet

PRETTY IN MY POCKET CASE STUDY

After working in marketing on the client side for years, Caroline van Sickle had somewhat of an epiphany about advertising: "The old way of creating revenue through advertising is banner ads, pop-ups . . . something that gets in the way of the consumers' experience. Online, on the phone, in a magazine . . . the experience tends to be intrusive. Instead of enhancing that content experience, you're taking away from it."

Two years ago when Van Sickle created Pretty in My Pocket (PRIMP), a mobile and social shopping platform for beauty brands, she wanted to make sure she was upending the conventional model in favor of meeting real consumer needs. One of the key consumer insights Van Sickle based her business on is that women tend not to buy beauty products from a single place: they mix and match high-end premium products with less expensive drugstore brands. Yet in spite of this, they don't have an easy way of making product decisions within the entire beauty ecosystem. In fact, as our Consumer Journey research confirms, consumers tend to get particularly bogged down in the Shopping stage at the shelf, with few tools to help them understand how products might be relevant to their unique needs.

For marketers, the challenge lies in meeting core consumer needs when there are both brands and retailers in the mix. Brands rarely have the opportunity to enter into direct conversations with consumers; they rely on retailers to capture consumer behavior information. Yet retailers face a tremendous number of logistical challenges as well, including finding the consumer in an increasingly fragmented landscape.

"Your customer is everywhere . . . that's the challenge brands have when finding her. It's not about the tech, it's about the fact that the next generation beauty buyer wants to buy from a drug store *and* a prestige brand, online and off. There's never been a solution where she could get information from all these places in one consolidated location."

PRIMP helps consumers choose and purchase beauty products by giving them access to reviews, tips, and content via photos, how-to videos, and featured content on mobile phones.

Van Sickle meets the needs of consumers by building a personal relationship with them over time, curating content from a community of beauty bloggers and experts. Beauty influencers or "Power Primpers" provide reviews and advice within their areas of expertise. "Makeup Mavens," a select group of women ranging in skin tone and taste, provide PRIMP users with information and advice from someone who looks like them—an ideal way for marketers to help support the personalization need we flagged up in the Consumer Decision Journey. Consumers can also unlock "Perks" (or coupons) for money off specific products. These perks are attached to contextually relevant content and have single-use codes for the purpose of retargeting if the consumer opts in.

For marketers, a backend SaaS technology platform enables brands and retailers to publish content and promotions that correspond to specific Universal Product Codes (UPCs), retail locations, and individual users. As consumers personalize their profile and use PRIMP's tools, Van Sickle's platform enables brands to make product recommendations within a contextually relevant environment—ultimately adding more utility and building closer relationships with their customers over time.

"Personalization is the new weapon; it's *the* tool," Van Sickle said. After all, consumers generally aren't interested in ads that are not relevant to them.

But Van Sickle also says that it's just as important to get a relevant message to consumers at the right time. Behavioral retargeting still isn't getting marketers there. "It's annoying when I'm online and now every ad I see has that Rag & Bone bootie that I looked at two days ago. When you've bought the bootie, you should stop seeing the ad."

That's where mobile comes in. While PRIMP is a cross-platform operation with a presence on every digital screen, mobile is their killer app; it enables consumers to pull in the content they need at the right time for them. "For mobile, you can have a one-to-one conversation. When you think of shopping for beauty products, even though e-commerce is on an aggressive growth trajectory, 80 to 90 percent of purchases still comes from in-store," Van Sickle said. "You can't bring a computer in with you, so it makes sense to have an app or mobile tool."

Van Sickle is not a believer in technology for technology's sake, however. "I don't think the app can stand alone. You need some anchoring element to establish relevance with the brands, retailers, and consumers." That's where additional platforms come in, including some very traditional ones. Point-of-sale material, public relations, social media, and e-mail all play a role in PRIMP's success.

Point-of-sale becomes increasingly important to link the in-store retail experience with the PRIMP app and its benefits. In New York City, Van Sickle piloted PRIMP with Walgreens and L'Oréal. PRIMP provided a customized code to "Primpers" for a L'Oréal Paris offer that could be redeemed at any Walgreens or Duane Reade drugstore in New York City. While there weren't any point-of-sale materials for the pilot, PRIMP's plan is to partner with retailers to include more POS material moving forward in order to increase consumer awareness of the app in the environment where it's most relevant.

For the pilot, the L'Oréal Paris coupon could be redeemed directly from the mobile app at the register. The coupon redemption data was subsequently coupled with analytics from PRIMP so L'Oréal could optimize performance for future offers.

Van Sickle's team also sees a tremendous amount of value from public relations.

A recent Despierta-America appearance increased new PRIMP users twenty times over average. Van Sickle also relies on social media platforms such as Pinterest to keep current users engaged, and finds that dropping personalized e-mail reminders now and then helps keep content top of mind.

According to Van Sickle, her average coupon redemption rates with national retailers are nearly 25 percent, significantly higher than the 2 percent average. "The true essence of being able to create a perk or a promotion within contextually relevant content that enhances discovery is the key," she said. "Then, once we've collected data and we know who this person is, we can partner with brands to surprise and delight her. For example, L'Oréal sent this perk, you redeemed it, and now we want to say thanks . . . here's another perk."

By meeting the personalization needs of consumers through reviews and timely, relevant content, while also giving marketers a channel to enter more personalized conversations with their customers, Van Sickle's model is changing up the retail landscape.

"Marketers must be so much savvier, but it's really based on a very core and age-old authentic relationship with your customer. That's it," Van Sickle said. "You create that trust and you have a method of talking to them on a regular basis that's not annoying—then, I'd say you've won."

Figure 3.7   Pretty in My Pocket Mobile App

Chapter 4

Introducing Quality Social

How to Harness the Real Power of Social across Screens

Humans are innately social beings. Almost everything we do is guided by our desire to connect with other people; social interactions are embedded in how we live, learn, work, and play. And many of the rules and conventions we live by are sanctioned by the threat of social ostracism—being cut off or shunned by the people around us.

When you think about modern society, our human connections are intricate webs that reflect the complexity of our contemporary lives within digital, virtual, immediate, and dispersed networks. In the past, social connections were relatively straightforward and typically defined by where people lived. The social nucleus was the family—mothers, fathers, children, grandparents, aunts, and uncles—who either lived together in the same cramped quarters or at least in the same town or village. In fact, in traditional cultures, this is still the norm. Neighbors and friends chatted over the fence, at church, and during community celebrations. Men (and it was typically men in those days) would forge social connections through their workplace. People created groups or associations based on hobbies, a shared sense of duty,

or passion for a common cause; quilting bees, service organizations like the Elks and Masons, garden clubs, and women's rights
groups were the foundation of many of these social networks.

By the 1990s, there was a growing school of thought that
people were increasingly turning inward, away from their community organizations, service clubs, and recreational groups.
Robert Putnam, who was one of the leading voices decrying the
atomization of society in the twilight of the twentieth century,
asserted that technology was a key factor causing social connections to wither away. In his book *Bowling Alone*, Putnam raised a
warning flag that social society was at risk as people increasingly
shut their doors to the outside world and sat in front of televisions
and computers until bedtime. Membership in service organizations, clubs, and guilds was on the decline as people spent more
time in their homes and divested energy in their broader community. The collapse of social society as we know it was probably
overstated, but it is hard to deny that technology in the 1990s
did not facilitate social engagement. Television had us flocking
to our homes instead of going out and engaging with friends and
neighbors at bridge clubs and bowling leagues. And the advent
of the computer meant that even at home, social engagement
diminished as we sat glued to our desktop screens, playing games
or surfing the new and intriguing World Wide Web.

When new things are on the horizon, old ways often recede
or disappear. And so it was with the evolution of social society
in the digital age. Social never disappeared—it just changed as
the world around us shifted from analogue to digital. The same
World Wide Web that engaged us in solitary virtual journeys
in the 1990s was suddenly our portal to new ways of socially
connecting, and not just with people in our immediate network.
Personal websites that others could visit and comment on, blogs,

online discussion groups, and virtual chat lines (to name a few) started to bring disparate people together to forge social connections, even deep friendships, without ever necessitating that people meet face to face. These smaller digital networks flourished for a short time, but quickly became replaced by bigger, macro networks: primarily MySpace and Facebook.

Interestingly, both MySpace and Facebook originated as smaller networks serving more intimate social needs. MySpace was a place where homegrown musicians could share music and connect with their fans. Facebook was famously a college network where Harvard kids could check out their neighbor or the girl they saw in chemistry class. But both networks quickly morphed into something else entirely, shifting away from their original purpose of forging connections between like-minded people. Instead, members sought to collect as many "friends" as they could by broadcasting out ideas, observations, and developments in their lives (big and small) and waiting impatiently for their 488 friends to comment.

Facebook has grown to be one of the biggest social networks in human history. The sheer immensity and global scale of Facebook has given it a key place in the media world. To capitalize on it, marketers have rushed to create Facebook identities for their brands, hoping to forge communities of brand advocates, collecting "likes" in the way ordinary people collect Facebook connections. Having 5,000 "likes" registered for a campaign or brand-driven activity has become akin to a metric for "making it" in the social stratosphere.

Twitter, the other social platform capturing attention in the media world, is more focused than Facebook creating communications channels between like-minded individuals. That said, success on Twitter is similarly measured by having millions of followers who take your observations or nuggets of intelligence and pass them around their vast network. Many consumers use it as a place to follow and communicate with people who have similar passions and interests, most marketers channel it as a mass network or broadcast communication channel.

Facebook and Twitter have become the foundation of what is defined as *social* in the digital age. While it is heartening to see the flurry of virtual social activity these platforms have generated, the downside is that many marketers have become reductionist in how they think about social: it is a platform-driven marketing strategy, a media buy, a commoditized "thing" that can be harnessed to build loyalty and buzz for products, services, and brands. This reductionism leads us to oversimplify what social actually is, and, even worse, removes the human element from something that is really the essence of being human.

Social isn't a platform or a campaign. It defines us through its expression in a multitude of ways and across channels, both physical and digital. Once again, in our quest to find simplicity in the complexity of our multi-screen world, we've taken a deeply human concept and lost sight of what it really means. We need to take a step back and re-set our understanding of social, and only then can we tap into the huge potential it has to connect people to brands in meaningful ways.

The Quality versus Quantity Conundrum

Social is such an immense concept that it's difficult to get concrete about how we tap into it as marketers. Given this, it's not very surprising that we've distilled down what social represents in the digital space so it seems more actionable. But, by doing this, we are missing key opportunities to use digital to ignite social in more powerful ways. Rather than aiming to simplify, what we really need to do is understand what underlies social behavior and how it manifests across screens. This requires asking why, digging deeper, and peeling back layers to get to the insight. We've learned that when we take the time to get a deeper understanding of human needs, clear patterns emerge, and these patterns actually start to drive a simple, yet effective strategy. So when we partnered with Pat Kidd at the Modellers to identify the fundamental goals people have when using digital channels, we were hoping to also get some insight about the role social plays within the context of these goals. We also wanted to get some precision around social: is it primarily a need, behavior, or goal? And how does it connect to our core values as human beings?

At the highest level, we find that being social is a fundamental goal that most of us share. But being social is not the end point—it is a means to helping us fulfill a set of core needs that we have as human beings. So what does this actually mean? As humans, we strive to be connected to our family, friends, and our social network—this is social as an overarching goal. Consequently, we make the time to talk on the phone, go out to dinner, e-mail, gossip over a coffee, or take a walk with people we enjoy. These social interactions, big and small, help us meet some pretty critical needs in our lives: to bond with people we care about, to help others, to have fun, to spend quality time with people, to create meaningful memories, and to achieve balance in our lives. As one person told us, "If I surround myself with people who bring joy in my life, I will simply live a joy-filled life. That means a life of fun, laughter, new experiences, and knowing I can rely on them if I need them."

When our social needs are met, we not only feel closer to others, we also feel happy and secure. In a world that is complex, busy, and stressful, we find joy in moments of connecting with others in big and small ways—the dinner parties with close friends where we reminisce over shared memories; the evening ritual of lying on the couch reading to our children; or a walk on a crisp autumn day with a loved one. These are the moments in our lives that renew us, balance us, and make life worth living.

We need to start reframing how we think about social—on a basic level, social interaction is a goal that we all strive to achieve. And digital has revolutionized the scope and scale of social interactions, making it easier to achieve our goal of connecting with others. But we need to go further. Social interactions also help us achieve deep and profound needs. If we can help people satisfy some of these needs, our brands, products, and services have the potential to drive loyalty, community, and advocacy that goes far beyond a "like." Once we start identifying consumer needs within the context of social activities we start to fully leverage the power of social.

Mass social networks have fashioned themselves after television: they argue that they deliver a Gross Rating Point (GRP)-like audience and create brand awareness around a community. But while television certainly does a fine job (creative permitting) of driving awareness and serving as a more enriching information source that connects consumers to brands, the same mass reach is contrary to what consumers need from social channels.

Through the intersection of digital and social, we've managed to facilitate mass social engagement. Facebook and Twitter are incredibly efficient at enabling us to meet our fundamental goal of staying connected to friends, family, and our social network. We can't always find the time to call, take walks, or go out for a drink with all the people we know and care about. These social platforms help us retain some level of connectedness that would be almost impossible in a world where our friends and family don't live in our immediate neighborhood or even city. Without having these digital means to connect, our friends in different time zones and hemispheres would eventually become distant pen pals or people we get in touch with a few times a year around the holidays or birthdays. In a funny way, these social platforms have become the modern-day equivalent to the letters people enclosed in our holiday cards, broadcasting out general highlights of our year and our children's amazing achievements. But, unlike these letters (which, I confess my parents and their friends still send out, much to my edification over the holidays), Facebook and Twitter enable us to send out mass communications in real time, not just once a year, which helps us achieve our goal of connecting with others in an immediate, tangible way. So, when I go on a trip to L.A. to attend my good friend Christian's wedding, I don't need to send out postcards to my parents and friends announcing that I'm in L.A., the weather is great, the wedding was spectacular, and we've had an amazing steak at Musso & Frank's. I just need to send a few posts to my Facebook account, detailing the great fun my family is having in L.A. The result? It's almost as though my friends are there with me, minute by minute. This is digitally enabled social connectivity on a massive, efficient scale.

But what I achieve in scale and efficiency, I lack in intimacy, personalization, and interconnectivity. So the payback for my flurry of L.A. posts nets out at 35 friends who "like" the picture of me enjoying a Mai Tai at Trader Vic's and 15 comments about the wedding venue. The fact is, while I'm scaling my communication to a huge quantity of people—mass communication, arguably—I'm not necessarily hitting the mark on quality. I'm documenting what I'm doing, and a few people might respond, but we aren't really having a dialogue or making a meaningful connection. So, while I'm arguably achieving my goal of connecting with friends, family, and my social network, I'm not necessarily getting my needs met through this scaled social interaction.

If we want to harness the true potential of Social, we need to move beyond facilitating scaled social connectivity and start helping people meet their social needs, including having a genuine dialogue with others, spending quality time with people, and achieving balance by being around those we care about and enjoy. This isn't just a call to action from us. Our research shows that people are seeking more meaningful, personal interactions with others, and they're turning to digital via laptops, mobile phones, and tablets to help meet these needs. And, these needs are not always getting met.

When we ask people to identify the different ways that digital helps them meet their social goals, interpersonal interactions and quality time with people they enjoy are flagged as areas that are important, but not being met by current platforms. A man we spoke to says, "Personal connections are important to me—being there when needed. A lot of my family and friends are back east, and being close is not always easy or doable, so communicating sometimes is difficult. Digital communications is not always 'personal,' and I usually revert back to the old methods."

"When it comes to being together, I want [it] to feel heartfelt and not so blank," says a Gen Y woman. "[I want to] have a more personal experience with people that involves emotions."

As these comments illustrate, the quality of social interactions matters to people. We need to start thinking about how we can facilitate conversations that are personal and more intimate.

Clearly, we have mastered the art of quantity, enabling people to broadcast their thoughts, ideas, and activities to lots and lots of people. We even measure our social success by the number of people we touch: likes, tweets, comments. But as that old chestnut reminds us: quantity is not necessarily quality. Let's explore in a bit more detail what "quality" actually means in practice.

The Power of Niche Networks

In 2013, our team conducted a global trends study with The Future Laboratory and IPG to track the ways in which consumers' relationships with technology are evolving. From March 2013 to June 2013, we interviewed 45 early adopters, men and women between 18 and 44 who are leading-edge technology consumers, across the U.K., United States, China, Brazil, Sweden, and the Czech Republic, to uncover a range of attitudes about technology and digital services. Then, we conducted an online survey with heavy Internet users in the U.K., United States, China, Brazil, Sweden, the Czech Republic, Russia, and Germany, with a total of 8000 consumers surveyed.

At its heart, Digital Trends explores the rapidly changing relationship consumers have with technology and the subsequent patterns that emerge. What we're quickly discovering is that these are not far-flung futuristic trends, but palpable consumer needs that can be observed at scale today. And one of these trends spotlights how social in the digital space is undergoing a significant metamorphosis—one that marketers need to be aware of now so that they can future-proof their multi-screen strategies.

Increasingly, people around the globe are moving away from the impersonal, meta-conversations that are the hallmark of social media today and turning to Niche Networks. A Niche Network is a smaller social network that enables consumers to fulfill needs, including bonding with others, spending quality time with others, and achieving balance in their lives. These connections are not made by broadcasting out messages, but by forging deeper relationships with like-minded people within the context of subjects they care about. In effect, people are choosing social engagements that emphasize quality over quantity. Wiser.org, for example, is a Niche Network that enables people to connect with each other over environmental sustainability, a topic that is not just a shared interest, but a passion for its users. Through Niche Networks, people are seeking more relevant, intimate, authentic social interactions in the digital space. And this isn't just a fringe movement: 41 percent of the people we interviewed across the globe are currently joining social networks that are premised on their specific interests and needs.[1] They are opting for meaningful interactions that are private, personal, and fulfilling.

If you think about the basic premise of *Bowling Alone*, people are reverting to a digital version of the world that Putnam fears has been discarded in the dustbin of history: the world of bowling leagues, stamp clubs, and gardening associations. But unlike our counterparts in the 1950s, who were forced to congregate in clubhouses and living rooms, we are now forging these networks in the digital space.

This desire for creating more intimate, meaningful, and relevant connections with others is echoed in other movements we're observing, including the shift toward "local" products or brands with "provenance." When we buy honey harvested by a couple of guys from Brooklyn with hives in their backyard, we are meeting the same set of needs that drive us to create a niche Manhattan Moms digital network. We want to feel connected to something real, tangible, and meaningful.

It is difficult to ignore the imprint of history in this swing back to "local" and "niche"—as soon as we hit a point where the norm is mass reach, consolidation, and scale, we yearn for a world that is more personal, decentralized, and intimate. And if we turn our focus back to the world of digital social networks, we can see that this trend toward niche started to manifest a few years ago. One early sign that there was movement away from mass networks was when we observed teenagers starting to get more selective about their Facebook friends, trimming their network down to the people who (for that week anyway) were their closest, favored friends. And as soon as Grandma joined their newsfeed, they ultimately switched to small networks of peers like SnapChat and WhatsApp. Ultimately, these smaller, more curated networks help get us closer to fulfilling the deeper social needs that we discussed earlier, including (but not limited to) having meaningful interactions, sharing important moments, and achieving a sense of balance in our lives.

If you think about how this plays out in practice, imagine the early days of being a new mom and dad. There is something terrifying and alienating about being home alone with a new baby—we are sleep deprived, anxious about doing the right thing, and are coming to terms with an exciting but significant change in our lives. One panacea for new parents is being able to reach out digitally to others. The world still exists outside of the confines of this home! But, at a certain point, it isn't enough just to broadcast out your thoughts, concerns, and moments of joy, hoping someone out there responds. You have specific needs: reassurance, support, and a deep desire to connect with others who understand. Finding a network of new parents whom you can relate to, turn to for support, and share experiences with becomes central to getting these core needs met. And, when these core needs are met, you are better able to cope, find balance, and truly benefit from the power of connecting with people with whom you have something fundamental in common.

This is the essence of a Niche Network. And if your brand, product, or service can become a fruitful part of this small community, you are in a powerful position to forge deep and meaningful bonds with your customers.

Introducing Quality Social

This brings us to the consumer-insights driven solution. We call it Quality Social, and it addresses core consumer needs and drives tangible value in three ways: it helps you find like-minded communities of consumers that align to your brand's attributes via niche networks; it provides an avenue to drive purchase or values validation; and it enables you to create word-of-mouth campaigns that are actually meaningful and relevant, and don't dilute your brand message.

Niche Network

First, let's tackle Niche Networks. How can marketers tap into these smaller networks across screens? To begin with, we need to move away from the notion that just showing up is meaningful—I have a Facebook page; therefore I have a social strategy. If there isn't a clear reason for your brand, product, or service to be involved in a network, then you shouldn't be there.

We also need to stop focusing on quantity over quality. It's not about having 5,000 friends, 145,000,000 re-tweets or 30,000 likes; it's about having the right friends, driving real impact and being liked by those who actually matter, the people who will cultivate loyalty and advocacy for your brand because what you offer is meaningful to them. In our Digital Trends study, we find that 53 percent of people are more likely to engage with a brand if it speaks to them on a personal level, addressing their needs and interests.[2] This means that marketers must be clear about what their brand, product, or service can contribute to a community. Membership must be earned! What value can you bring to the network that gives you the right to join?

Imagine that you are a small business that offers personal training services, and you are trying to attract new mothers who are busy, but desperate to get back into shape. You can't just show up and invite yourself into the new parents' network we spoke about earlier. *Hey, ladies! Get rid of that Mummy Tummy for the low price of $85 per hour!* Imagine if you shift your thinking from selling to supporting. Instead of peddling your sessions, you offer weekly tips on nutrition and how to ease back into an exercise routine, and offer realistic goals and timeframes for getting your pre-baby body back in the absence of a personal chef, five nannies, and a live-in trainer. By being a valuable member of the community and addressing the core needs of these new moms, you become the "expert" and trusted advisor. And by clearly demonstrating your value, you get value back—customers who proactively want to bring you in because you are making their lives easier or better in a tangible way.

It is also critical to be an active member of the community. You can't just show up as wallpaper and hope that your presence is enough to generate buzz and conversation and then subsequently propagate a network. Marketers must ensure that they are genuinely participating in the network in a meaningful, additive way. In the new world of Quality Social, it is critical to think about building reciprocal relationships, not just critical mass. Adding value to niche networks can range from offering ongoing tips and support like the personal training business to making experts available for one-on-one dialogues with community members when they want guidance. The possibilities are endless: financial service companies providing seminars to help new investors manage their portfolios; home improvement stores with experts on call to help people whose amateur forays into plumbing lead to a waterlogged ceiling; food and beverage companies that provide customized advice when people are throwing a party and aren't sure how much to buy and what to serve. If you are clear on why your brand, product, or service is meaningful and additive to consumers, then you already have the road map for becoming a valuable, contributing part of a community.

Finally, the core of these niche networks is driving advocacy among the right people—those most predisposed to love, or at least be committed to, your products and brands. Having 350,000 friends, followers, and likes is not the endgame. It is better to have 2,000 close friends who are willing to follow you into the trenches than 350,000 who are here one day, gone the next. As marketers, we strive to build communities of loyalists and advocates who are passionate about our brands and products. Typically, loyalty and advocacy are established when a brand or service intersects with a consumer need and a relationship is established. Niche networks offer targeted opportunities for brands to proactively establish these relationships.

At their foundation, niche networks are forged because members share a set of core interests—getting in shape, being better cooks, investing for short-term gain. When a brand or product can align with and meet the network's needs, a relationship can be quickly established with people who are predisposed to want what is being offered. And by delivering what consumers want time and time again, trust is won, and loyalty and advocacy follow. The value of niche networks lies in the opportunity to preach to those who will be most easily converted. And once conversion happens, these consumers become advocates, bringing other like-minded consumers into the brand family. The starting point for a quality-focused social campaign across screens is grounded in establishing meaningful connections between people to help them achieve social needs like belonging and supporting one another. But it's also about finding the quality people who are going to be the most influential and effective conduits of your message.

Purchase Validation

In addition to tapping niche networks to drive quality social interactions, the second way marketers can help consumers address key social needs is when they are making purchase decisions.

In Chapter 3, we laid out the consumer decision journey framework in detail and talked about the importance of external validation in the Experiencing stage of the journey. Once people buy whatever it is they set out to get—shampoo, snacks for their kids, a television, or a car—they take the product home. This launches the final stage of the consumer decision journey: Experiencing.

At this stage in the decision journey, two key things are happening. First, people expect that when they try their new shampoo, drive their car for the first time, or turn on their new HD television, the product will deliver against whatever promise led them to make the purchase in the first place. So if I want a volumizing shampoo, then it had better make my hair full and lustrous; if I buy a fuel-efficient car, then I'll want to see more mileage to the gallon; and, if I get an HD television because I want amazing picture quality, then I expect to see vivid, true-to-life imagery on the screen. But despite the fact that we believe our job is mostly done if our product delivers against its promise, people need more if they are going to become true advocates and brand loyalists. To consolidate loyalty with a brand and drive social engagement, people require external validation from others that they've made the right purchase decision.

What does external validation mean in practice, and how does it help us get clarity around how to drive a quality-focused social campaign? At the heart of external validation is having other people confirm for us that we bought the right thing, which triggers confidence and satisfaction with a purchase. Once again, our social needs emerge as critical, even when doing something as basic as buying something.

Imagine buying a new car and over the course of a year, not one person tells you that he likes it. We might actually question whether we've made the right decision. What is the point of having a beautiful new car if no one notices? But flip this situation around. You've just bought a new car and your friends come over and admire it in your driveway. A few days later, you're reading the autos section of your local paper on your laptop, and there is a feature article praising the car you just bought as one of the most fuel efficient on the market. Then, you happen to be browsing consumer reviews on your tablet, and you see that almost everyone who purchased this car over the past year gave it a five-star rating. All of these different streams of communication converge and give you the confidence that you made an excellent decision when you bought the car. Not only do my friends think it's amazing, but experts rate it, and other people who bought it think it's great. This validation from others is critical to solidifying my relationship to the brand and product: I am more likely to talk about the car to others (advocacy) and also more likely to buy this manufacturer's car again (loyalty). Loyalty and advocacy don't necessarily come from being attached to big social networks or having lots of friends. They come from helping people feel good about their purchase decisions and giving them the confidence that they made the right choice when they bought your product or brand in the first place.

So how do you support or even orchestrate external validation as a marketer? A good starting point is by doing something as simple as helping people connect with others who have also bought your brand or product and want to share their experiences. This can include serving up opportunities for people to access product reviews immediately post purchase to see how happy others are with their purchase or soliciting on-the-spot feedback that immediately gets shared out with others. Another good way to drive validation is to provide people with expert help immediately after they buy something; experts can provide post-purchase support to ensure people have a great early experience with a product. They can also help sanction the purchase by offering advice, dialogue, and affirmation.

Think about buying a case of wine. You may have a glancing understanding of the differences between a Sauvignon Blanc and a Pinot Grigio and hope that you've bought a selection of wines that you won't be ashamed to serve at a dinner party. But, once you get home, you aren't sure whether you should serve the Vignoier with fish or chicken and whether you need to decant the Pinot Noir before pouring. So much uncertainty! Imagine that when you open up the wine case, there is a card enclosed with a QR code that you scan with your mobile phone. Upon scanning, you're able to access a site that allows you to set up a quick video tutorial with a wine expert who can walk you through your case, offer serving suggestions, and advice on what to chill, let breathe, or convert into a Sangria. Suddenly, you are armed with the necessary knowledge to serve the wine in a competent fashion—which means a better overall product experience—and you are also far more confident that you've made a good choice because an expert has sanctioned your selection. At the heart of external validation is deploying social in small, but meaningful ways to help people meet a basic need to have their purchase validated. When consumers feel good about a purchase, it can drive loyalty and advocacy over time.

There is also a big opportunity to create a richer, more prolonged external validation experience by proactively building a Niche Network around your brand, service, or product. We think a lot about perpetuating our relationship one on one with consumers post-purchase by sending deals, follow-up e-mails from sales associates, or e-mails about related items that might spark interest in an additional purchase. These activities may stimulate another purchase, but they don't help people meet their need for post-purchase validation. So instead of focusing on the brand-to-consumer relationship, creating a Niche Network involves putting consumers in touch with each other, with the brand playing more of a supporting, facilitating role.

All of the rules of Niche Networks apply in full force here: the brand must clearly demonstrate the value of joining the community, actively participate as an authentic member, and create a culture of reciprocity where value is exchanged. It's not about being an outsider looking in, but playing a vital, meaningful role as an integral part of the community. Marketers must continuously give members a reason for joining and staying involved, which can involve creating virtual or real events to bring the community together, offering special insider opportunities or deals, inviting experts to provide advice or product support, and creating forums for discussion, sharing, and advice. The key point is that all of these different activities and engagements, facilitated by the network, provide regular, ongoing affirmation to consumers that they made the right purchase and are part of a group of happy owners. They fulfill consumers' need for post-purchase validation from others. This is the essence of external validation, and it's an opportunity for marketers to drive a quality-based social campaign that helps people meet core needs and generates loyalty, advocacy, and repeat purchase in return.

Spider-Webbing

Finally, a third opportunity for marketers to drive Quality Social emerges from a study we conducted to understand the core needs driving people's multi-screening behavior. We've seen a lot of studies documenting how people move across screens, usually starting with the television, then picking up other devices like the mobile and tablet in a roughly simultaneous fashion. All the screens are on and actively being used at the same time. But to what end? When we dig a bit deeper, we discover that one of the needs that people are seeking to fulfill when they use multiple screens is fundamentally social in nature, specifically, all of these different screens are being used to help people reach out, share, and connect with others. Digital is once again emerging as a great conduit to help people meet their need of having quality social interaction with others, with each screen allowing for easier, more seamless connectivity and engagement between people. We call this simultaneous pathway Social Spider-Webbing.

Social Spider-Webbing is typically ignited with a content catalyst. The most frequent is still that largest of screens—television. Consumers see something that sparks their interest, and this drives a desire to share ideas, thoughts, comments, or opinions around what they've seen or heard. It is tempting to assume that the key to Social Spider-Webbing is to land something provocative, funny, or startling on television (or another screen), which will generate a flurry of social buzz. Mass sharing of content and getting thousands of people to view your video or campaign is better than nothing; at least you aren't throwing content into the wind. But isn't it better to have the right people sharing your content with others in a meaningful way? Social buzz isn't meaningful if a message is increasingly diluted—or worse, subverted, as it spider-webs across screens and along varying strands of content (vines, videos, tweets). The objective is to have your message validated, reinforced, and perpetuated among people who are advocates and genuinely influential.

To do this well, marketers need to create clear alignment between what they want to say and what people want to hear. With television advertising, this is an old art that most marketers have mastered. But in the world of digital, we're often focused on gimmicky content that gets passed around because it captures immediate, short-term attention. It's very possible that Kelly may have forwarded me a YouTube video of animals jumping on trampolines when she was supposed to be writing today (and equally possible that I watched it!), but I couldn't tell you which brands were advertised within the video because they had absolutely nothing of value to offer in that small moment of distraction. Like a fireworks display, this sort of approach generates a big burst that lights up the sky, yet minutes later, all that's left is smoke.

As marketers, we should aim to generate multi-screen social campaigns that mobilize around a clear need and drive meaningful, additive sharing and connecting. The ideal outcome is to cultivate loyalty and build lasting consumer relationships with our products and brands. To limit the potential of Social Spider-Webbing to driving awareness and sharing without impact is to remain entrenched in the world of Quantity Social.

Increasingly, our energy needs to be deployed into creating campaigns that are Quality Social at their core. We've suggested three ways to launch Quality Social campaigns today: through niche networks, by providing post-purchase validation and by orchestrating Social Spider-Webbing campaigns that pivot around a need and drive genuine impact. These approaches are just the tip of the iceberg. If we are willing to take the time to understand the needs that underpin social interaction, we'll uncover a spectrum of opportunities to create social campaigns that are meaningful, resonant and have staying power.

It's always instructive to watch the marketers who are getting it right. The case study below illustrates how a company that's been around for nearly a century harnessed the power of quality social to create a slow-burning campaign that leaves more substance than smoke in its wake.

CASE STUDY: LA MARZOCCO

A beautiful product. An Italian heritage. A passionate following. Some companies have all the luck. But La Marzocco, an espresso machine maker founded in Florence, Italy, faced a big challenge in 2013. How would they take their most iconic, beloved product, the La Marzocco Linea espresso machine, and get their customers to accept and upgrade to their new and improved model?

The La Marzocco Linea has been an icon of specialty coffee since its release in 1990, and first became well-known when Starbucks leveraged it during their initial, and eventually very *vente*, retail expansion. The Linea was so good, in fact, that even after being in production for nearly 25 years, with only minor technical updates and no design changes, it remains La Marzocco's most popular product. The new La Marzocco Linea PB, charmingly named after the original designer, Piero Bambi, refashioned the classic look of the original while adding a new advanced interface software system that enables more temperature precision, as well as other technical updates that have come to market since the Linea Classic's introduction in 1990.

With fewer than 10 marketing employees worldwide and an estimated installed base of 13,000 Linea Classic machines in use around the world, Marketing Director Whitney Cornell had her work cut out for her. But she also knew that in order to get her customers to re-up their legacy machines, she had to tap into something more emotional than just the features and benefits of the new model. Like most of Seattle-based Cornell's good ideas, this one came to her in her sleep.

"We're a legacy company, we've been making espresso machines since 1927, so the stories that we have to tell are rich. We thought about it as re-making an icon," Cornell said. "It was sort of like re-launching a classic car. Our customers grew up with these machines. Some baristas learned to make coffee on them and then obsessively saved their tips so they could buy one and go out on their own. So it seemed we should let our customers tell *their* stories."

For many of Cornell's target audience, which include resellers and influentials in the coffee business—roasters, coffee equipment technicians, baristas and the like—the Linea holds a tremendous amount of affinity for its owners and the people who work on them every day. So rather than espouse the technical features of the new Linea PB, Cornell and her team decided to create a campaign that tapped into a more emotive quality through the very best niche network they could find: their own La Marzocco Linea customers.

Cornell and team invited the specialty coffee community to share their fondest memories of the Linea and what it meant to them. Titled the *Linea Love* campaign, the program leveraged the mobile-friendly tumblr platform and the hashtag #linealove. Cornell hired a small agency to do the creative, but she didn't invest in any paid media. Contributors were encouraged to use whatever medium helps tell their stories best: writing, drawing, video, pictures, even songs and poems. The response was nearly overwhelming.

"We were almost immediately getting submissions from all over the world," Cornell said. "We could curate and post them to the site. We even use these stories at our events."

Cornell's team recognized submissions and followed up with thank you gifts featuring the Linea Love campaign graphic: a red heart surrounding an image of the Linea espresso machine. Contributors and customers were sent T-shirts and stickers. "We started seeing the T-shirts show up everywhere: on Instagram, Twitter, and in industry publications. Customers who received the Linea Love stickers came back to us asking for more branding. They wanted the La Marzocco brand on there!"

And as you might expect, the Linea campaign, so close to the hearts of Cornell's customers, is just about perfect for the mobile phone Lover archetype. "Tumblr renders really well on mobile. Many of our influencers—baristas—are accessing the site and sharing their stories from their mobile phones," Cornell said.

Cornell attributes the success of the campaign to her team's ability to move beyond a functional "features and benefits"-driven marketing plan, and instead, reach their customers on the devices and through the channels that enable the emotional benefit of the product. "The experience of coffee, the ritual of preparing a beverage, is a very intimate experience," Cornell said. "In some ways, there's an intimacy between the barista and the machine, and between the barista and the customer they're serving. The vehicle for facilitating that connection *is* the espresso machine."

One only needs to read the stories on LineaLove.com to see what she means:

> I remember the first time I worked on [a Linea]. I approached with caution . . . how did I get the opportunity to use this modern wonder? Surely I was not ready, this had to be beyond my knowledge base. I quickly accepted that I had reached the Rubicon and disengaged the portafilter. The grip felt so comfortable and natural. There was such a refreshing simplicity to everything: the clean lines, the EE switch, the aha! moment of learning gradual steam pressure. Any concern I had, dissipated. This was a machine that I could use, learn with and grow on.
>
> Now as I embark on my own coffee venture, I feel lucky and excited to begin my business with a Linea. It is almost an unwritten rule that those of quality start with it. . . . It's going to be a lot of fun.[3]

Cornell said, even now, the campaign has a life of its own.

"We wound down the active campaign around the end of May, with the introduction of the Linea PB in Australia. And still, you'll see that people are continuing to use the hashtag

#LineaLove," she said. "This is like gravy on top because the community is owning the campaign, and as the Linea PB is adopted, the campaign continues to benefit the brand."

The success of the campaign has inserted new life into the Linea legacy. But Cornell still faces challenges as a small business owner.

"There are moments when I feel overwhelmed. We all contribute to the social updates, from our four offices around the world," Cornell said. "But we're not a company that can post nine times a day. We'll go dark for a few days. If it's not authentic, it bombs, so I encourage my team not to force it."

Cornell's campaign yielded two big lessons. The first is especially resonant with business-to-business marketers. "There *can* be emotion in business communication," Cornell said. By letting her own customers tell their Linea stories, Cornell tapped into a powerful niche social network centered around real human emotion: nostalgia, as well as pride in quality and ownership.

Second, she let social media work for her, rather than designing a program where she felt like she had to work for social media. Just like any human interaction, when a conversation topic is authentic—that is, your brand shows up in a community where what you stand for is relevant—the conversation flows more naturally. Quite simply, Cornell says, "Our audience tells us what works."

It's worth noting that The Consumer Decision Journey is evident in both Chapter 2's Yezi Tea example as well as La Marzocco's case study. Yezi Tea, as a company just staring out, is investing heavily in the Open to Possibility and Decision to Buy or Change stages; they need to break open a new audience and get them to buy. La Marzocco, however, has been around for a long time; they have a strong network of passionate existing customers. As a result, they're able to invest more heavily in upselling

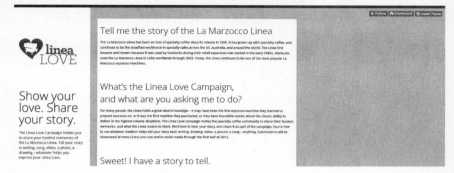

Figure 4.1   The Linea Love Campaign

their current customers in the Experiencing stage in order to bring them around to additional and ongoing purchases, while also acting as brand advocates to bring in new customers. Finding the right Niche Network is a critical way to drive Quality Social in order to facilitate brand affinity as La Marzocco was able to do authentically and affordably via the Linea Love campaign (see Figure 4.1).

CHAPTER 5

Simplify Your Multi-Screen Content Strategy

IT'S TIME TO RETHINK "CONSUMERS IN CONTROL"

It doesn't take a particularly keen observer to recognize that consumers are bombarded by data, information, and advertising on just about every available surface. Some of these surfaces are brand-new, and yet we rush to monetize them as if they were just another billboard-sized image on the side of a city bus. Marketing today evokes an almost dystopian image of a world resembling Times Square: giant screens filled with grinning faces and garish phosphorescent headlines assaulting people as they stumble down the street bewildered by the noise, lights, and messages coming at them from all directions. At home, on the street, on the subway, in our cars, even at work, we're exposed to advertising content, be it via television, radio, mobile, tablet, out-of-home display, or even on the backs of our shopping carts.

How can people possibly filter through this information without losing their bearings? What should they pay attention to, think about, and act on, and what content can they blissfully ignore?

As marketers, we have mixed emotions about this information overload: we feel a bit guilty since we're perpetuating this situation as content creators and owners, but at the same time, we worry that our messages will get lost in all the noise. Maybe we should shout louder than our competitors or make sure our messages appear on every screen at all the key moments in a consumer's day. Or perhaps make the ad unit spin! But in spite of our tricks, we ultimately realize that you don't win consumers' hearts by bombarding them with advertising. So how do we help consumers navigate through the noise to land on the right message on the optimal screen that drives the results we're looking for?

From "Always On" to IntelligentlyOn

It seems like only yesterday when our clients were asking us to help them be "Always On" (in fact, it probably was). *Consumers are always on—we need to be, too.* And while for most marketers that's meant crafting content that can be easily pulled in from any screen wherever consumers are, it also means seeding compelling ideas that are easily discoverable for consumers. But we're seeing a new trend of late, recently revealed in our Digital Trends 2014 research, led by our colleague Anita Caras and conducted in partnership with IPG Mediabrands and The Future Laboratory. This is a trend Anita calls *IntelligentlyOn*.

What if technology understood consumers' context and mood, and knew when to speak up and when to be quiet? For example, texts are automatically turned off when you are driving your kids to school in the morning. Or of social networks are programmed to shut down when it's time to meet one's multi-screen book deadline (that last example is completely random, of course). In our busy lives, technology can heighten feelings of information overload and chaos—and people are starting to resent it. We recently saw a panel of women in New York led by

Arianna Huffington and were shocked to hear the same message resonating over and over again: "Technology has helped me be successful, yet I resent having to be 'always on' and it's starting to ruin my most important personal relationships."

Consumers are seeking time away and looking for a compromise between being "always on" and switching off. In fact, according to Future Poll's Consumer Attitudes Audit, 47 percent of consumers want to spend time away from the Internet. Take a look at luxury resort marketing as an example. Ten years ago, they advertised having Wi-fi and enabling the ability to connect while you were away on vacation. Now, top resorts advertise their *lack of Wi-fi* and connection with the outside world—that's *real* luxury now. Consumers can change the settings on their phone so that updates only come through at certain hours of the day. This means no more e-mailing in bed or texting over dinner. We see that 55 percent of global online consumers are interested in future technology that can predict when users want or need to be connected and respond by switching on or off. And 46 percent of global consumers are already aware of digital devices and services that offer filtered messages, calls, alerts, and content at different times in order to give more quiet and peaceful moments.[1]

Technology should intuitively create a clutter-free and productive way of living. Not always off. Not always on. *IntelligentlyOn*. Marketers need to tune in when their audience needs them most, or there won't be anyone listening. This means learning when to disappear and how to make every interaction necessary. Keep communications simple, minimal and relevant.

LESS IS MORE

The IntelligentlyOn trend signals a big shift in the way we think about marketing. Since the onset of social media, marketers have gotten more and more comfortable with the idea of "consumers in control." And, in fact, many marketers have gotten so comfortable that they happily bombard consumers with more content, more advertising, and more choices, expecting them to filter through it all on their own. But by giving consumers control and expecting that they will naturally navigate through complexity to find what they want, we're actually doing them a disservice. We need to stop and ask ourselves, *Are consumers really in control?* And, in fact, perhaps the more important question is, *Do they really want to be in control?*

By giving consumers control, we are actually shirking our responsibility as marketers. We bombard consumers with too much information, too much data, and too much advertising, but we try to solve the problem by assuming consumers will take matters into their own hands and gravitate toward what they want and need. On a basic level, we've allowed ourselves to believe that by providing people with a marketplace of ideas and information, they can pick and choose what is meaningful to them. People are too smart and savvy to embrace a brand or product just because we advertise that it's perfect for them.

But have we stopped to think about what control actually means from a consumer perspective? To begin with, consumers by nature pay attention to what is relevant and shut out what's meaningless to them. Every human being with control over his basic faculties can ignore a pop-up ad for a miracle weight loss drug or daydream about a beach holiday when a dull commercial appears on the television screen. Tuning in or out is a very rudimentary notion of control.

At the other end of the spectrum, giving consumers the freedom to sort through information and find what is relevant is actually the reverse of control. In fact, we are making an assumption—and a big one—when we think that people have the time, energy, or desire to curate their own content. First of all, information gathering is not a hobby; it has a distinct purpose, which is to help us make better, more informed decisions. And when you consider the sheer number of decisions we need to make over the course of a day or week—what to buy, where to eat, how to invest, when to exercise, or whether to visit a doctor about that nagging shoulder pain—it is inconceivable that people want to plough through vast quantities of information to find the relevant piece that will help them make the right decision. If anything, having too much information to wade through makes people feel *out* of control. When deciding whether to send my daughter to public or private school, I don't want to plough through 15 articles on the top schools in New York, 25 expert blogs on navigating the school application process, and listen to 12 opinioned friends with differing views. Buried in all that information may be the seminal piece, but the idea of wading through and finding it exhausts and overwhelms me.

As marketers, we need to think about providing people with just enough information to enable faster, easier, and better decisions. As Mies van der Rohe famously said, *Less is more*. Too much information bogs us down, impedes decision making, and makes us feel out of control. But if we have the exactly the right information we need to make a good decision, we feel in control. A study in the *Harvard Business Review* affirms the importance of information simplification: "The single biggest driver of customers' likelihood of following through on a purchase, buying the product again, and recommending it was, by far, 'decision simplicity,' the ease with which consumers can gather trustworthy information about a product and confidently and efficiently navigate their purchase options."[2] Brands and products that help people make faster, easier purchase decisions by providing useful information will enjoy advocacy and loyalty as a byproduct.

When we explore consumer decision making, we typically find that consumers struggle to get their information needs met when making purchase decisions, even for simple purchases such as shampoo, laundry detergent, or skin care products, despite the plethora of information at their fingertips. We believe the onus is on marketers to take control and help consumers find the information they need. And we can't just make assumptions about what we think people want. When I'm standing at the hair care shelf at my local drugstore trying to decide what brand of shampoo to buy for my sun-damaged hair, I don't want an e-mailed coupon for a straightening product or a salesperson to come by and upsell me on an expensive deep conditioner. I want access to information that helps me find the product that will best fit my need and appeal to my mind-set at the moment. To deliver relevant information, we need to roll up our sleeves and take the time to understand our consumers on a deeper level: What are their goals, and what do they need to hear from us? Making the effort to do this means that when consumers buy our products and brands, they feel confident that they've made the right decision, which is the real essence of consumer control.

There's some good news for multi-screen marketers in all this. Your content strategy doesn't need to be nearly as complex as you might think. There are two steps to simplifying your multi-screen content approach. The first is to facilitate discovery by seeding simple, curated content on relevant screens. The second is to craft that curated content around your audience's fundamental goals as it relates to your brand.

FACILITATING DISCOVERY IN DEVELOPED MARKETS

In our 2012 study *What Moves You?* conducted with Ipsos OTX, we set out to learn how consumers discover content and what makes them act on it. One of the key findings was that consumers *want* marketers to take control of the flow of information and messaging. They feel overwhelmed by the sheer volume of content out there and believe marketers should step in and help them navigate a path through the clutter. As one of our male respondents in the United States told us, "For a company to successfully engage me in something, they must first not waste my time with too much information. That's the biggest turnoff."

In our study, we found that consumers in developed markets like the United States and the U.K. want advertising content to feel serendipitous. In other words, they want the illusion that they have just stumbled across the information they need at the right time and on the most relevant screen. It's important to point out that consumers are not naïve or operating under the false assumption that all of this happens coincidentally or magically. They know that they are being targeted and that marketers have invested the time to understand their needs and behavior in order to serve them up the right message at the right moment. Sharing data to receive personalized, meaningful, useful information is particularly valuable to consumers. It enables streamlined decision making and helps us feel more in control of our complex lives.

As our good friend Shelley Zalis, the CEO of Ipsos OTX says, it all boils down to IWWIWWIWI. Translation: *I want what I want when I want it.* In other words, help me land on information that is relevant to me at the right moment. When marketers help consumers get it right by delivering "serendipitous" advertising—that is, curated messages that are personalized and meaningful—consumers are three times more likely to pay attention to the message we're conveying.[3] This is all pretty intuitive stuff—meaningful messages capture consumer attention. But it goes deeper than just capturing attention. Marketers are actually in a unique position to help simplify and streamline the information people need to get things done and make decisions they can feel good about. It is in our power to help consumers feel more in control—ironically, by giving them less of it.

Case Study: Jay-Z's *Decoded* and Bing: A "By the Book" Serendipitous Encounter

A great example of a serendipitous advertising campaign that very literally had people stumbling across meaningful content in the right place, on the right screen, and in the right moment was a Bing campaign supporting the publication of Jay-Z's book *Decoded*. Let's get one thing straight: Jay-Z is cool. His people are not going to come up with a bad advertising campaign. But what really resonates with us on this one is how well executed it is across both traditional and digital channels. And even better, it is an excellent example of how marketers can take back control in order to give consumers curated content and a feeling of serendipity.

The *Decoded* campaign included more than 300 pages of Jay-Z's book to decode, 600 traditional, nontraditional, and digital advertising placements in 13 cities around the world, and within Bing Maps, 200 contest winners and a multimillion-dollar budget. The marketing goals were threefold: to increase Microsoft's relevance with the Y generation audience, engage more consumers with Bing's new mapping software, and generate buzz about the then-new Jay-Z autobiography. By taking pages of *Decoded* out into real-world locations and by creating an online experience using social media technology, the execution hit the sweet spot with Generation Y. Produced by creative agency Droga5, the treasure hunt utilized transmedia storytelling, or the art of telling stories across many different media platforms and formats, in order to drive online interaction and offline purchasing.

Here's how it worked: Every day for a month, a new page of Jay-Z's book was placed in a different U.S. or global location relevant to the content of the page. The pages were displayed on unexpected objects—reimaging the idea of what a surface or screen can be—such as an old Cadillac parked on a street in

Brooklyn to commemorate the birth of New York Hip Hop, the pool tables at Jay-Z's 40/40 Club, the lining of a leather Gucci jacket, and even the bottom of the Delano Hotel's pool. The different locations of each page allowed Bing Maps to show off its capabilities through the execution itself—a terrific example of "showing, not telling." With the creative inspiration from Droga5, Microsoft designed an interactive website for the campaign that encouraged consumers to follow the pages as they were released and to build the book online free of charge. A clue to where a page would be released was given each day via the website and Jay-Z's Facebook and Twitter accounts. And everyone who located a page was entered into a contest for two tickets to see Jay-Z and Coldplay in concert at Las Vegas on New Year's Eve.

As you can imagine, the agency's main challenge was to bring together the product (Jay-Z's memoir), the sponsor (Bing), and the audiences. But rather than overwhelming consumers with the technical capabilities of Bing Maps or the same old sound bites and reviews for Jay-Z's memoir, they capitalized on the concept of curated experiences, leading consumers to an experience that felt serendipitous, yet was actually quite simple in execution. In its first month, the campaign drove an 11.7 percent increase in visits to Bing, according to Microsoft's internal numbers, with an average engagement per player of 11 minutes. The campaign earned 1.1 billion global media impressions. Ultimately, the book hit the best sellers list for 19 weeks and even the agency got into the act: Droga5 won a Grand Prix Lion (Cannes Festival) in the Outdoor category in 2011.

And here's how it was deceptively simple: all the content for the campaign was already in the book and within Bing's mapping capabilities. The marketers didn't need to come up with new flashy content; they already had it. The execution was all about leading consumers through the content via moments of serendipitous discovery.

FACILITATING DISCOVERY IN EMERGING MARKETS

Emerging markets like China and Brazil offer a few new challenges for marketers. In both countries, there has traditionally been less authoritative content, and the emerging middle class is still new to many global brands. As a result, consumers still need help navigating through the morass of information, messaging, and advertising that is out there. But unlike their counterparts in developed countries, who expect marketers to guide them to the right content, consumers in China and Brazil rely on friends, family, experts, and influentials to take the lead. As one of the consumers we spoke to in China says, "Using technology to keep in touch with friends and family is essential. It's social and fun, but also how I get information before making decisions."[4]

There are a number of reasons that the opinions found on social networks, both close in and further out, are so central to decision making in emerging markets. At a macro level, as we discussed in Chapter 2, consumers in emerging markets can be wary of information from "official" sources, including advertisers. The closer in the source of information—and the more personal it is—the greater the level of trust in its veracity. Similarly, in many emerging markets, family, community, and social connectedness are central to people's way of life. Generally speaking, extended families live close together, communities are tight knit, and interpersonal connections trump individuality. So, having a friend, colleague, or an influential like a news host or doctor talk about the superior quality of a cleaning product or a face cream has a big impact on a consumer's decision to buy.

We find this pattern across most studies we conduct in emerging markets. In China, 80 percent of consumers trust recommendations from friends and family, 62 percent seek out expert options, and 64 percent look for validation from consumer reviews when making purchase decisions.[5] We find that even for habitual purchases like home care or personal care products, 27 percent of Brazilian shoppers rely on their social networks and consumer-driven newsfeeds for information, compared to 17 percent of their global counterparts.[6] And for higher-consideration purchases like cars, we see the same pattern play out. In India, personal connections are highly influential when buying a car, with 60 percent of buyers relying on their partner or spouse's opinion and 56 percent turning to consumer review sites for information and advice.[7] In fact, many of our respondents even took their entire families—grandmothers and all—on their test drives.

So when marketers want consumers in emerging markets to connect with their products and brands, it is critical to facilitate opinion sharing among friends, family members, experts, and influentials. These social networks help consumers sort through the mass of messaging and information to land on what they perceive to be "quality" information. And landing on the right information to ease decision making helps consumers feel more in control because their decisions have been sanctioned by information from people they trust. There are wide-ranging ways marketers can do this:

- Using mobile apps or in-store digital screens to enable access to consumer reviews that influence purchase decisions through the sanction of fellow consumers.

- Giving new buyers the opportunity to share their views through e-mailed links or apps that can be downloaded to facilitate post-purchase sharing.

- Connecting consumers to experts or influentials through blogs, tweets, digital articles, or streamed videos to provide trusted information and validation to help with purchase decisions.

- Building communities or niche networks of consumers with the brand as sponsor or intermediary to stimulate regular dialogue, support, and advice around the product or brand.

At the core, all of these marketing activities offer a way to connect consumers with people who can share information to support purchase decisions and help consumers in emerging markets feel that they've made the right choice. This is the foundation of giving consumers a feeling of control. The brands that facilitate this will eventually become as trusted as the people whose opinions helped give consumers the confidence to buy in the first place. Here's an example of a global brand that built a niche network to create an authentic relationship with consumers in emerging markets that are genuinely customer first.

CASE STUDY: VW, THE PEOPLE'S CAR PROJECT

Volkswagen has always built cars for the people—practical, affordable, and reliable, making it a brand that appealed to consumers' sense of rationality. In fact, in German and Chinese, Volkswagen means *the people's car*. But when Volkswagen expanded into China in the early 1980s, the brand faced a unique challenge.

After a period of unparalleled growth for some two decades, by 2010, China was producing 13,897,083 cars per year,[8] 24 percent of total global volume. Consumers could choose from more brands and models than anywhere else in the world. At this time, Internet and mobile technologies were also developing at a tremendous rate. All of these previously unknown choices meant consumers faced new challenges in their purchase decision making. In a market with a first-time car buyer rate of still some 60-plus percent, "word of mouth" from family and friends and information from digital and social media became important sources of information. Due to Volkswagen's long history and people's perception of the brand as a maker of reliable but less aspirational cars as it related to design and technology, Volkswagen was challenged to overcome its image as a practical, yet somewhat uninspired choice.

To change this perception, Volkswagen initiated its "The People's Car Project" in 2011. Knowing that Chinese consumers, 620 million of whom are online,[9] typically approach and discover brands through their social communities, Volkswagen created the ultimate social experiment: They engaged consumers in the co-creation of new concepts for future auto mobility.

Rather than creating a static website or social media page, Volkswagen, together with their partnering agencies, wanted to ignite consumer imagination by holding a two-way dialogue in which consumers became actual innovators of the future. They had big goals, but they also had limited time and a constrained budget, with only 15 percent of the media spend for a typical car launch, and just a little more than a year to prove they were effectively lifting brand perception. They needed to be just as efficient and agile as the brand they were championing.

Volkswagen and their agency decided to create a curated "dialogue platform" where consumers could click their way to co-developing their dream car by posting ideas, images, and videos that were discussed and further developed by other consumers in the community. Volkswagen engaged five major social networks (Sina Weibo, Kaixin, RenRen, QQ, and Douban), allowing users to join the program and seamlessly share content they created within their own communities.

To increase the quality of user-generated ideas, relevant content was seeded into passionate communities (designers, car fans, techies, travelers, moms, and so on). Volkswagen also integrated platform voting and creation functionality into those same communities to drive deeper engagement.

Upon launch, paid media generated massive awareness and response. Owned and earned media sustained activity through the announcements of new campaigns and the presentation of the best ideas from previous campaigns:

- Out-of-home TV-generated mass awareness
- Viral videos kick-started the online conversation
- Web-TV episodes sparked engagement on video-sharing sites
- Members and social network fan bases drove advocacy
- Online, mobile advertising and search engine marketing (SEM) sustained repeat platform visits
- Guerrilla stunts inspired mass online buzz
- Car show exhibitions and quarterly events showcased the best ideas to journalists, opinion leaders, and the public
- Media celebration of The People's Car Project design car created by Qinghua University students added additional authenticity with a young, influential audience

The best and most unique ideas were regularly passed to Volkswagen engineers and designers to provide user feedback and to develop sketches and concepts. These concepts may be adapted into current cars and will influence future car development. In the course of this process, three innovative and highly consumer-relevant product ideas surfaced: the "Hover Car," the "Smart Key," and the "Music Car."

Wang Jia, a designer in China, leveraged the insight that she faces an incredible amount of traffic on her commute. She wanted to create something that would help ease congestion, rather than exacerbate the problem. Her suggestion: a hover car. And, in fact, Jia's design came to fruition. The Hover Car, an environment-friendly two-seater city car that hovers just above the ground, is a zero-emissions vehicle that could in the future travel along electromagnetic road networks.

"The creative ideas from The People's Car Project give us valuable insight into the needs of Chinese consumers," Alexei Orlov, CMO at Volkswagen Group, China, said. "The trend is toward safe cars that can easily navigate overcrowded roads and have a personal, emotional and exciting design."

The "Music Car" serves the need that many consumers expressed for more unique and individualized designs, as well as more advanced interaction with their surroundings. Equipped with organic light-emitting diodes, the exterior color of the "Music Car" changes with the driver's choice of music. The car becomes a means of self-expression and a fashion statement for young drivers. This was a positive way to win over a fickle, design-conscious millennial audience.

The final winning product idea was the "Smart Key." The "Smart Key" integrates online technologies seamlessly into the vehicle: the slim, 9-mm key has a high-resolution touchscreen that keeps the driver up-to-date on gas consumption, climate conditions, and the car's security via 3G network. The driver can also monitor the vehicle from a bird's-eye perspective through real-time satellite transmission.

Not only did The People's Car Project change perception of the Volkswagen brand in a challenging market, it also helped influence new models with consumer needs at the core: the need for agile, environmentally friendly models; the need for personalized design that lets young Chinese consumers express their personalities; and the need for smart cars that leverage technology to connect consumers through data to gain a better understanding of their vehicle and how they use it.

In the end, the campaign was incredibly successful. The website received more than 14 million unique visitors, 0.4 million registrations, 0.5 million followers, inspired 0.25 million ideas, and achieved 36 million The People's Car Project video views.

Volkswagen was also voted most innovative by 70 percent of people surveyed[10] and was perceived as the number one brand in China.[11]

"With The People's Car Project, we are listening very carefully to what our customers have to say," Orlov said. "Brands to my mind that truly succeed, understand the importance of relevant dialogue, generous steering and most important, fully appreciating that one of the most important elements of communication is not just to hear—but to listen—and take heed."

Clearly, it is our responsibility as marketers to help consumers land on meaningful content that facilitates decision making. As a starting point, we need to acknowledge that the concept of "consumers in control" has very little to do with empowering people to tune in or out of content or giving them the freedom to hand pick what is relevant from mountains of information. Consumers, regardless of where they live, want shortcuts and guideposts to help them land on what is worth paying attention to and what they can safely ignore. At the core, being in control is about making smart decisions with the right information. In developed markets where individualism is valued, consumers want marketers to provide them with a reduced set of meaningful, personally relevant choices to expedite decision making. And in emerging markets where community and connectedness are valued over individualism, consumers want people whose opinions they trust and value to help them discover the right information to make good decisions. Once again, it's important to note that every market is unique; these are general guidelines to follow as you develop global marketing campaigns.

So how do marketers actually help consumers find the information that is right for them to make easier and better decisions—whether through serendipitous discovery or trusted social or niche networks? As a critical starting point, it's about aligning information and content around what consumers are trying to accomplish, their goals, and the needs that underpin these goals. In other words, it's about taking the time to understand the "why"—consumer goals and needs—behind the "what"—the content, information, and data consumers seek on the path to making purchase decisions.

DETERMINING YOUR AUDIENCE'S GOAL-STATE

Now that we are clear that consumers want access to relevant, additive content we need to determine which types of content will resonate with them in alignment with your brand and marketing objectives.

In the fall of 2013, we partnered with Pat Kidd at The Modellers to do just this—identify the foundational goals consumers have that drive engagement with content and explore the core needs underpinning these goals. We leveraged laddering—a technique that moves consumers through a series of questions that start with function and evolve to reveal more emotional needs—to understand not only what consumers hope to accomplish through online channels, but also what needs are served by the digital content consumed across screens. While consumers are reasonably conscious of their goals, their needs are a little harder to pin down. If a consumer's goal is financial security, for example, what deeper and more emotional need does this goal serve? And how do marketers that provide financial services use screens to move beyond delivering diffuse, one-size-fits-all content to serve deeper and more unconscious needs?

As we mentioned in Chapter 4, our research, known as Microsoft's Goal-State Model, identifies nine universal goal-states that are relatively consistent (though incidence varies) in the two markets we studied, the United States and Brazil. These fundamental goals include:

1. Taking care of family and loved ones

2. Being healthy and well

3. Gaining financial security

4. Finding support through social interaction

5. Achieving spiritual or religious well-being

6. Participating in things greater than oneself (charities, etc.)

7. Having fun and being entertained

8. Learning and being educated

9. Finding ways to express oneself through creativity

These nine goals show up in the ways we engage with digital content nearly every day. We believe the bridge between these goals and the needs they serve represents a strategic opportunity for brands and businesses to craft communications that connect to consumers in more personal and very human ways. And creating this kind of content will give consumers the information they need on the right screen, in the right moment, to make better and faster decisions—which is the essence of serving up curated content to make decision making easier.

Knowing a consumer's goal is a critical starting point. Then, as always, we need to continue to ask ourselves *why* consumers are trying to achieve this goal. If you market for a local bank in Columbus, Ohio, financial security is likely going to be the goal for nearly all of your customers. But financial security can be underpinned by wide-ranging and variant needs: having nice clothes, jewelry, and an apartment filled with beautiful things (status); being able to retire early and play golf in Palm Springs (quality of life); or providing your children with an excellent education (being a good parent). Without understanding *why* someone is striving for financial security, it is pretty challenging to know what type of content and information to provide. Imagine the big miss if you develop a campaign around the "finer things in life" and send it out to people who are trying to spend less so they can send their two kids to college. Pinpointing these needs is essential if our goal is to provide people with relevant information to help them make better decisions

It helps to think of this model like a sandwich; it simply wouldn't be the same if any ingredient were missing. The consumer goal is the bread; ostensibly, it's the essential reason why a consumer consciously embarks on the path to a decision. The condiments are the activities the consumer engages with to meet this goal. But the filling—meat, peanut butter, or sardines—is the basis for sandwich; it's the deeper need that consumers are consciously or unconsciously trying to fulfill around the broader goal. Without the filling, a sandwich isn't really a sandwich—it's a couple of slices of bread.

To move from the world of delis to the world of marketing, without a core need shaping your content, you are just contributing to the mass of diffuse information, messaging, and noise that consumers have to sift through—which is pretty far removed from helping consumers feel more in control. Let's look at an example.

Health and wellness, the second-most-mentioned goal in our Goal-State Model, begins with activities: searching for product ingredients, reading about different kinds of exercise, researching supplements, looking for healthy recipes. When you ask consumers why they are doing these things—*Why are you searching for different types of aerobic exercise on your mobile? Why are you reading an article on your Tablet about Vitamin D?*—consumers move beyond describing activities to articulating the rationale for their behavior. The answers you might hear could range from *finding the optimal exercise to lose weight quickly to getting in shape to run a marathon in the spring;* or *looking at whether I need additional supplements in the winter to understanding the role of vitamins in autoimmune diseases.* Now keep going. *Why are you running a marathon? Why are you concerned about autoimmune diseases?* The answers within this set of questions— *feeling a sense of accomplishment; the peace of mind that comes from managing a newly diagnosed chronic illness*—provide a depth of understanding around the precise content needs of these consumers.

So while exploring vitamin supplements, exercise routines, and healthy snacks are all different activities that lead consumers to engage with content across screens, they coalesce around a deeper, and divergent, set of emotional needs. The goal of health and wellness ultimately reveals four foundational needs: peace of mind, family security, a sense of accomplishment, and happiness. Brands that help consumers meet these needs by delivering relevant content across screens will be more useful to consumers—and ultimately more successful—as a result of fulfilling these fundamental needs. Why? Because they provide consumers with meaningful, useful content that not only helps them make decisions that are critical to meeting important goals—but makes them feel more in control in a complex, often stressful world.

So a small company selling healthy snacks might create a mobile app (we've learned from Chapter 2 that mobile is the most personal device and well set up to enable on-the-go utility) that helps people find which local health food stores stock their product. But they're also going to make sure it aligns with a key consumer need within the health and wellness goal-state: peace of mind. So to truly add value to this interaction using digital content across devices, the company enables this mobile app to not just help people find healthy snacks, but also facilitate the emotional need—peace of mind—by providing lists of product ingredients and the health benefits (or risk reduction) of each snack. When consumers go to their local health food store and buy the snack food, they are confident that they've made a smart purchase decision because they've bought something that has ingredients that will help them control their blood pressure, achieve weight loss goals, or increase fiber intake.

Table 5.1 illustrates how each goal-state (the bread) ladders up to fundamental needs (the filling) and down to the activities

Table 5.1 Consumer Goal-States

Goal	Needs	Examples of Digital Activities
Taking care of family and loved ones	• Family security • Close companionship • Happiness	• Posting photos to SkyDrive on a laptop • Skype chat with grandparents via tablet app • Planning a family vacation online using TripIt via laptop
Being healthy and well	• Sense of accomplishment • Peace of mind • Happiness • Family security	• Wear a fitbit to track sleep and fitness • Use a calendar on a laptop to keep track of doctors' appointments • Save healthy recipes in a Pinterest folder via a tablet
Gaining financial security	• Peace of mind • Family security • Sense of accomplishment • Prosperous life	• Track spending habits on Mint.com via laptop and mobile • Invest money using a Fidelity app on laptop • Check account balance on mobile banking app
Finding support through social interaction	• True companionship • Peace of mind • Happiness	• Sharing photos on Instagram via mobile phone • Sending an e-mail to an older friend via Outlook.com on a laptop • Joining a support group online via tablet
Achieving spiritual and religious well-being	• Peace of mind • Salvation • Happiness	• Subscribe to a daily poetry site delivered via SMS on mobile • Watch spiritual seminars or sermons via a video site on a tablet

(continued)

Table 5.1 Consumer Goal-States (*continued*)

Goal	Needs	Examples of Digital Activities
Participating in things greater than oneself (charities, etc.)	• Sense of accomplishment • Peace of mind • Happiness • Self-esteem	• Signing a petition online via laptop • Sending e-mails to local representatives or congress-woman via mobile • Sending money to Kiva via mobile app
Having fun and being entertained	• Companionship • Vitality (exciting life) • Happiness	• Playing Spotify on mobile • Watching Netflix on Xbox One • Playing a game with Xbox Kinect
Learning and being educated	• Family security • Sense of accomplishment • Wisdom (mature under-standing of life)	• Watch a TED talk on a tablet • Use Bing to search for essays, lectures, or online classes
Finding ways to express oneself through creativity	• Happiness • Vitality (exciting life) • Sense of accomplishment	• Singing up for an art class online via laptop • Using video software to create movies • Searching the web for inspiration

(the condiments) that people engage in around each goal. It also pinpoints the specific screens consumers use to meet these needs. You can use this model as a jumping off point to identify which goals are salient to your product or company so that you can target the underlying needs of your customers on the right screen.

Once you understand the deeper needs you want to target in alignment with your marketing strategy, you can help consumers find the right information to make decisions and help them achieve their goals. Whether this is done directly by advertisers or through networks of families, friends, coworkers, or experts, marketers who can make consumers feel more in control of their lives by helping them arrive at faster, more informed decisions will create deeper, more reciprocal relationships with their consumers.

As we've learned, it isn't about taking a step back and letting consumers run the show—it's about partnering with consumers, understanding them on a deeper level, and making their lives easier. We all know that marketing in the digital age should be about dialogue and reciprocity. To do this, we need to make the effort to get to know our consumers, their goals, their needs— and we need to take control of the information we provide to them, especially as screens proliferate and complexity increases. The ultimate responsibility lies with marketers to give consumers the confidence and control they seek.

CHAPTER 6

Drive Efficiency by Targeting Consumer Needs, Not "Millennials and Moms"

LEARN THE MULTI-SCREEN AUDIENCE TARGETS THAT MATTER

The digital marketing world has a new obsession called *Programmatic*—the practice of triggering marketing campaigns based on a set of data-driven algorithms. This approach might include real-time bidding through ad exchanges, site retargeting, shopping cart abandonment campaigns, dynamic creative optimization, and even the sort of product recommendations on online shopping sites that are served up based on past purchases. Programmatic campaigns can be triggered by a number of different actions, from consumer demographics—age, gender, income, and often location—to online behavior.

For digital marketing, targeting is all about focusing on the audience that matters to your brand, and eliminating those audiences that don't—ultimately making your marketing dollars more efficient. So as programmatic marketing moves to a multi-screen universe, the inevitable question arises: *How do I target my audience seamlessly across screens and then measure the effects of my media?* In other words, how do I know I'm getting the right audience and that my marketing is resonating with this audience on all the screens they use? We'll tackle the measurement question in Chapter 5; here, we're going to focus on audience targeting.

Any kind of audience targeting comes down to a fundamental question: When we buy media, what are we buying? Traditionally, we've bought mass audiences and the possibility of those audiences viewing and engaging with ads showcasing our product or service. Whether you buy an ad displaying expensive watches in the *New York Times* Style section (hoping to reach affluent men) or a banner ad for your car dealership via the online version of the *Main Street Gazette*, media companies offer up a package and plan based on an audience demographic. Marketers—and media buyers, in particular—optimize media based on budget, type of medium (radio, Internet, TV, print), quality of the medium (target audience, time of day for broadcast, etc.), and how much time and space is wanted. Since the dawn of television, we've targeted traditional demographics that make up a combination of men or women, as well as age ranges: 12+, 18–24, 35–54, 55+. For local buys, perhaps we'll layer in geography and a few psychographic attributes as well.

For years, this approach has worked. Selling hand soap? Target women ages 24–54 who do the household shopping and watch daytime TV. How about a family car? Put an ad in the paper for dads 24–54.

But here's the rub: it isn't just women doing the household shopping anymore. And consumers aren't getting their information from a 30-second soap spot on daytime TV. The world has changed, yet media companies are still selling the same old audience profiles associated with their services. So why are we buying them? When it comes to multi-screen marketing, buying audiences in conventional ways is obsolete. But the irony is that even as we add efficiencies through innovations like behavioral targeting—arguably better—we're still missing the multi-screen demographics that really matter.

THE CHANGING NATURE OF DEMOGRAPHICS

As you can imagine, there isn't just one trend driving the need to change the way we buy audience-driven media. For our purposes, we'll focus on three major forces precipitating this need: first, increased access to homogenized information through globalization and the flattening of traditional localized demographic distinctions; second, the fluid and changing nature of demographics based on recent economic and societal shifts; and finally, the fragmentation of mass audiences as they consume media across multiple screens.

Let's start by touching on a topic that could fill this entire book if we let it: the flattening of global culture. The convergence of technology and the globalization of economies have fundamentally changed how populations around the world access information. Women in Saudi Arabia are reading American gossip magazines online; popular U.K. television shows such as *Downton Abbey* have hit the United States, Canada, Australia, and Europe; teenagers in India are playing Jay-Z on their mobile phones outside Mumbai train stations; everyone everywhere can access Wikileaks. And it doesn't take long to figure out that at the core, the *Real Housewives* of Athens, Greece, aren't all that different from the heavily bejeweled ladies running amok in New Jersey.

Thomas Friedman's *The World Is Flat* accounts for the tilt toward increasing globalization with a list of Ten Forces, two of which are critical factors in the changing nature of marketing: "Uploading," the practice of communities around the world

collaborating through blogs, software, and content that proliferate through platforms such as Wikipedia, and "the Steroids,"
personal digital devices and utilities such as mobile phones, computers, instant messaging, video, and now tablets.[1] As content
becomes a commodity and technology gets cheaper, consumers
around the world have access to the same information—be it
entertainment, political, commercial, or social in nature. These
global citizens can create, collaborate, compete, and share with
others from diverse cultures, religions, educational backgrounds,
and languages. As a result, we are sharing more than ever before.
Simply reducing people down to a location with a few stereo-
typical attributes isn't going to give you enough information to
accurately identify an audience as appropriate for your brand.
Your best customer may no longer be in your backyard—or even
in the same country as your current customers.

In some ways, globalization can be positive. African farmers
with access to cheap mobile technology and the myriad information it provides are able to check weather patterns and make
adjustments to their crops, yielding more food and economic
success in their communities. But despite the world getting
smaller with some subsequent convergence of human behaviors,
we shouldn't oversimplify the effects of globalization. As any self-
respecting Canadian (that would be Natasha) will tell you, we
still need to be sensitive to and account for differences that exist
across countries and cultures. In the global consumer insights
work we do, basic human needs are more similar than different
around the globe, but the context for these needs is complex,
nuanced, and can subsequently make or break a global marketing
campaign. If you are a global marketing organization, you should
leverage local experts to stress-test creative, copy, and strategy to
make sure it works in your target market. That includes other
countries or even more rural regions within the same markets.
But the bottom line is that as culture proliferates through the

Internet, borders are disappearing, and most marketers will need to change their approach in order to keep up.

Let's take a look at the second factor that contributes to this shift away from traditional media buying demographics: the changing nature of demographics due to societal and economic forces. Natasha's father, who is about to turn 80 (but don't tell him we said so), is a world traveler, active hiker, and freaks out if he misses his thrice-weekly gym workout. My dad is 63 and spends more time geeking out at the Apple Store and download-ing new apps to his iPad than his Microsoft-employed daughter would like to admit (though he loves the Lenovo all-in-one with Windows 8.1 he got for Christmas!). Similarly, my mom shops at LuLu Lemon and is obsessed with Pinterest. These aren't our grandfather's retirees. Boomers are living longer, more robust, and healthier lives with more income to spend on travel, technol-ogy, cars, housing, yoga gear, appliances, and more. And yet this is the age group traditional media-buying demographics have relegated to a very undesirable and unspecific 55+. We cry foul (and so do our dads!).

Similarly, there's a distinct shift among women, a very tradi-tional consumer packaged goods and retail target, moving out of the realm of home and childcare into the working world. They're not necessarily abandoning one for the other, but their needs are certainly changing. Women make up half of the U.S. workforce, and the number of stay-at-home mothers is declining. And while American women still trail men in science, engineering, and busi-ness, women are now earning more advanced university degrees than men. Among adults 25 and older, 10.6 million U.S. women have master's degrees or higher, compared to 10.5 million men.[2]

Additionally, a Pew Research Center report confirms that marriage continues to lose market share; according to census data, half of adults ages 18 and older in the United States are married, compared to 75 percent in 1960. The age at which men and women marry for the first time continues to rise, as well. In 2011, the median age for a first marriage is an estimated 28.7 for men and 26.5 for women. In 1960, the median age for a first marriage for both men and women was in the early 20s.[3]

And this is not just a U.S. trend. In Latin America, where large families born to young women was the historical norm, a similar pattern emerges. A more educated female populace and an emerging middle class is contributing to women delaying having children and having fewer kids when they do. Between 1970 and 2000, around 30 percent of Brazilian women aged 25 to 29 were childless; by 2010 the proportion had risen to 40 percent. In Peru, childlessness among women of that age group rose from 26 percent in 1993 to 33 percent in 2007.[4]

Better education and delayed motherhood means women have the ability to spend money on themselves and make head-of-household financial decisions, both when they are single and if and when they get married and have children. As a result, a 45-year-old single female in Chicago may be living the same lifestyle as a 23-year-old single working woman in Bangalore, while a 43-year-old mother in Manhattan may have a nearly identical lifestyle to a 21-year-old with a young child in Brazil. So why are we still using traditional demographic targeting for women and moms? It's time to rethink traditional demographics and look at more meaningful signals to target audiences. Here's an example of a marketer who has.

Xbox has traditionally been thought of as a medium for young males. Advertisers such as Doritos, the U.S. Army, and the video game maker Electronic Arts have lined up to advertise on Xbox because it's one of the rare places where teenage boys are actually engaged. They don't watch much television these days, but they play a lot of Halo 4. Intuitively, it made sense.

But Xbox isn't just for teenage boys anymore. A full 40 percent of Xbox users aren't men at all; they're women.[5] And they're not just playing Halo. They're also streaming video and using Xbox's social functionality to connect with friends and family. So what appeared to be an ideal opportunity to reach young men turns out to be an even better opportunity women. In 2012, L'Oréal capitalized on this insight with a very nontraditional media buy.

L'Oréal teamed up with Xbox 360 to create an app tailored specifically to women. Titled "The Next Level," the app features tiles with daily style tips, how-to videos, articles and beauty- and style-focused entertainment. Consumers can interact with the app on a personal level, getting advice from a personal beauty assistant as they earn "style creds" toward special offers from L'Oréal. The app is unique in two ways. By making the app available on the Xbox, L'Oréal brings a level of interaction and engagement that wouldn't otherwise be achieved via mobile or tablet apps. Second, as voice and gesture control become more and more ubiquitous, consumers will be able to not only bring brands into their living rooms, but interact with them on a more natural and personalized level.

What does the Xbox/L'Oréal example tell us? It is nearly impossible for marketers to use traditional demographics to target their audiences as they move from screen to screen. We can't make assumptions about who is on which screen based on gender, household composition, or even behavioral data. As a result, it's harder to find your customers across screens, let alone serve up the right information that's truly meaningful to them.

This brings us to the third reason we're seeing a demographic shift. The traditional notion of mass audience is changing. Must-see TV is more like DVR-TV. And even those mediums and live events that do attract mass audiences—the World Cup, for example—aren't being consumed on a single screen. Media is more fragmented than ever before, and as a result it's becoming more and more difficult to scale mass audience targeting across screens. Whereas just 10 years ago, millions of consumers watched primetime television, now that time is divided among several screens. According to recent Nielsen data, 75 percent of smartphone and tablet users are engaging with second screen content more than once a month as they watch TV. And about half of those people are engaged with second screen content daily— that's about 50 million people.[6] Primetime hasn't gone away, but it's no longer happening in one place among a large audience. In fact, according to our research, 64 percent of consumers agree that they would find it difficult to watch television or a movie for two hours without picking up a second screen.[7]

In our 2013 Cross-Screen Engagement study, we identified four common multi-screen pathways. These pathways represent screen combinations that consumers use for multi-tasking, investigating, sharing and connecting with others, and for productivity. When we look at the proportion of people engaged in each of these four pathways, we don't see a lot of differences across the markets we studied, illustrating that *what* humans do is more often than not similar. But when we break these pathways down by demographics, some interesting patterns appear. These patterns are less about age and gender differences and more about the specific needs driving the multi-screening behavior. For example, younger consumers have fewer adult responsibilities, so they spend more time making social arrangements and engaging with friends online. But new moms and dads spend nearly as much time online with their social networks, usually so they can get tips from other new parents and get a little adult conversation while they're at home with their baby. So while the behavior among young adults and new parents might look the same, the motivation is very different. The meaningful differences that help you target consumers are not found in the *who* or the *what*; once again, they're found in the *why*.

As our analytics tools continually get better, it is becoming easier to target digital behavior. Behavioral targeting is arguably better than straight demographic targeting. But it can still misfire. I've purchased more than my fair share of baby gifts for friends' showers, but don't have a child myself. Yet I'm constantly served up ads based on past visits to baby sites. My need for baby gear is based on one-off gift giving, not ongoing interaction with these brands, so when baby companies target me with motherhood messages, they've got the wrong gal.

Behavior is a better place to start, but as an industry, we need to take it to the next level so that we can understand the motivations behind consumer behavior. So how do we do it? *What if we stopped trying to target demographics and behaviors and started targeting consumer values and needs instead?*

Behavior versus Needs

If you follow consumer research these days, you're likely to see plenty of studies that are full of facts about how different audiences behave in the multi-screen world. Millennials use mobile phones. Moms use social media. Men play video games. The intent of these studies is to further our understanding of what specific consumer audiences are doing: what content do they engage with and on what screen? But as we explain in the first chapter, it's even more essential in an increasingly fragmented media landscape to uncover *why* they're doing it. And this comes to the fore when understanding demographic behavior. In our Cross-Screen Engagement study, we go beyond assigning percentages to the number of people using two screens simultaneously to actually understanding why they're on both screens. This enables us to not just identify which screens specific audiences are using, but also helps us uncover their motivations for doing so. Understanding these motivations gives us more insight into where to place media and how to craft messages that will be relevant within these multi-screening moments. Let's take a look at the difference between *behaviors and needs* using the Cross-Screen Engagement study as an example.

The first multi-screening pathway is what we call Content Grazing, where different or unrelated content is consumed on two or more devices simultaneously. This is the most common multi-screen path, with 68 percent of consumers across the five markets we studied[8] engaging in this behavior. If we stopped here, we might come to the conclusion that a lot of consumers are using multiple screens to multi-task, and, therefore, we should catch them in this behavior with content that is productive in nature. *They're busy, they're using devices to get things done— let's help!* But before we start to develop marketing strategy based on what we see people doing, let's take it a step further. When we dig deeper to understand why, we discover that 47 percent of Content Grazing consumers are not really multi-tasking, they're just flitting from device to device out of habit. And when we look at the content consumers are pulling up in this pathway, it's less about getting things done and more about entertainment— playing casual games, texting friends, and watching short, entertaining videos (see Figure 6.1). Thus, the motivation here is less about productivity and more about using a second device to assuage boredom. This is distraction behavior at its finest, so our original assumption to go with productivity-oriented messaging couldn't be further from the truth.

The second and third pathways are what we call spider-webbing, where consumers engage with related content on two or more screens simultaneously. Spider-webbing has two different need-states underlying it: investigative and social. Investigative spider-webbing is fairly common, with 57 percent of consumers

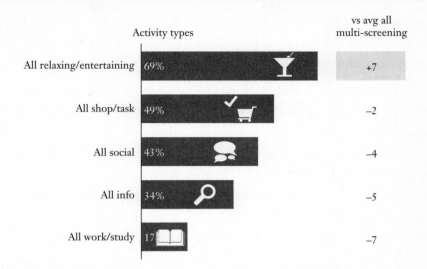

Figure 6.1 Top Activities within the Content Grazing Pathway

seeing a piece of content on one screen that sparks their desire to investigate on a second one.[9] Each thread of the web represents a line of inquiry that the consumer pursues. Imagine that you see a television ad for a Tesla and it piques your curiosity, so you turn to your tablet and read a Wikipedia entry about the Tesla to find out more.

With social spider-webbing, 37 percent of consumers see a compelling piece of content that drives them to share with others through a second screen.[10] In this instance, each thread of the web represents a different stream of communication or sharing that stems from that initial piece of viewed content. You may be watching television and see an ad for a great fare deal to London, so you pick up your mobile and tweet it to your friends. You also grab your tablet, and send out a message to some friends to see if they want to join you for a long weekend across the pond— umbrellas mandatory.

The last pathway is called Quantum, where consumers embark on a cross-screen journey over time to get a task completed: 47 percent of consumers engage in this real multi-tasking behavior,[11] where they have a specific need and use different screens to get this need satisfied, whether it's finding a restaurant for dinner or buying a new pair of pants.

Within our pathway data, we're able to break down each of the four multi-screening motivations by specific audience segments. When we do, we see key differences emerge in the motivations driving each pathway. You may have a product that appeals to both male and female millennials, for example, but the motivations driving how they use each screen are different. As a result, you'll want to adjust the way you drive content for millennial women versus millennial men.

Here's an example: When we look at Figure 6.2, we see that millennials in general are more likely to engage in social spider-webbing. And we also see that over 81 percent of women under 55 are among the most active on this pathway, illustrating that this is a mainstream behavior among younger females.[12]

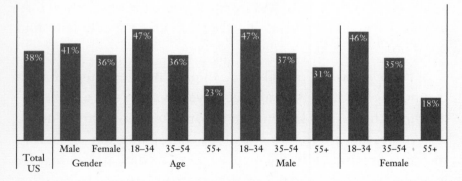

Figure 6.2   Social Spider-Webbing Incidence by Age and Gender

But key differences emerge when you look at the motivations driving social spider-webbing for men and women. In Figure 6.3, you can see that while enjoyment is key for female millennials, motivations such as control, recognition, and power are higher for males. Brands that want to spur men to share and connect their content therefore need to shape it very differently

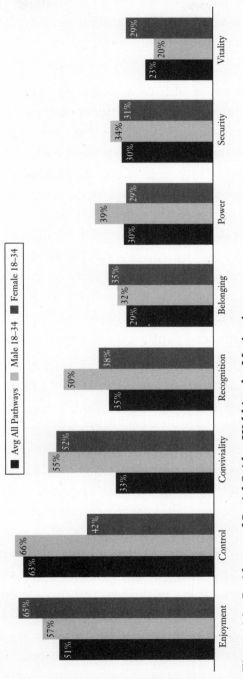

Figure 6.3 Incidence of Social Spider-Webbing by Motivations

Legend: Avg All Pathways | Male 18–34 | Female 18–34

Enjoyment: 51%, 57%, 65%
Control: 63%, 66%, 42%
Conviviality: 33%, 55%, 52%
Recognition: 35%, 50%, 38%
Belonging: 29%, 32%, 35%
Power: 30%, 39%, 29%
Security: 30%, 34%, 31%
Vitality: 23%, 20%, 29%

from the way they would for women. The example that follows will show you how you can drive content against these motivational differences.

Let's look at an example of how a campaign would look different based on buying traditional audience demographics versus a needs and values-based approach. If you own a sports apparel store and want to be associated with the World Cup, you can take two approaches. The first is the traditional demographic approach: you want to advertise your store on television during the World Cup, and based on behavioral data, you know your customers are also likely to be using their mobile phones while watching the event. So you run a local TV ad publicizing your store during the televised match and you also purchase mobile display ads based on the same demographic profile as your TV buy: men ages 18–34. You might layer in some behavioral targeting for efficiency and also capture men who have visited a FIFA site in the past six months.

Now, here's an alternative approach. Rather than going with the traditional television demographic cut, you focus on the needs of your customer. You know from prior engagements that your customer base is predominantly male, but they typically watch with partners who are also enthusiastic about the game. They love watching live soccer and especially enjoy the social nature of the event. Their primary needs are to be socially engaged while watching the match; to access easy communication channels in order to discuss the ups and downs in real time with their friends; and to have fun, relax, and enjoy the moment. So rather than purchasing a television-and-mobile buy based on TV demographics, you focus on your customers' needs: they want in-the-moment fun and real-time social engagement. And according to our cross-screen cut, the men in your target audience might also like an element of competition that brings them control and recognition.

Next, you align your brand objective to the consumer need: you want them to associate your store with a sense of fun, and ultimately purchase sporting apparel to make matches memorable. You also want to drive loyalty by helping consumers capture the singular experience of the event that will be over all too soon when the game ends and they need to go back to mowing lawns and doing laundry. Similar to the first example, you know they'll have their mobile phones at the ready while watching the television screen, but you also know that since the motivation is social and fun in nature, they're not going to be paying attention to tiny advertising banners popping up on their mobile phone. So you decide to sponsor a game that enables your customers to stay in the moment of enjoyment, share with friends, but also relive the fun later. So here's what you do:

Leverage the social spider-webbing pathway and run a "World Cup Moments" campaign where you sponsor a contest incentivizing your customers to take pictures of themselves and their friends using their mobile phone during the match. These photos will unlock pieces of information they can share with their friends—being "in the know" and appealing to that recognition or power motivation many of the millennial men have. Customers post these photos with your store's hashtag, and they get 10 percent off their next apparel purchase, plus automatic entry into a 500 euro gift card drawing. Because the motivation or consumer need is social in nature, you run your ads around social tools on mobile phones—Facebook, Twitter, Outlook, and Skype—reminding consumers of your brand and the benefit they get from interacting with it in the very places where they're engaging with others. The result? Deeper engagement and relevance to your customers' needs and values.

So now we know why the way we think about traditional demographics needs to change. What do we do about it? Clearly, many adjustments need to be made in the ways that media is bought and sold. At Microsoft, we're experimenting with new, more personal forms of digital marketing and finding more relevant methods to reach audiences to monetize that reach. We'll share more on this in Chapter 7. In the meantime, however, there are tactics that marketers can activate now to target the right audiences across screens and get smarter about reaching and engaging them.

FOUR STEPS TO DEFINING YOUR NEW MULTI-SCREEN TARGETS

We believe there are four distinct steps to defining your multi-screen targets. Following these steps can help drive multi-screen marketing campaigns that are less dependent on old media segments and more relevant to the audiences that are really buying your products and services. The key point here is that layering these four steps incrementally will help drive better, more effective targeting.

First, define your audience segments. Who are they? What are they doing? Where are they showing up? This is where you'll take your knowledge of your customer and combine it with analytics or insights that help inform where you need to be. This step is primarily about incidence. If you're a long-term care insurance company targeting seniors, you'll want to know whether seniors are using multiple screens. If so, which ones and in which combinations? If you're selling psychedelic nail polishes to teens, you'll want to know where they're spending their time online. Which screens are dominant? And how are they using them together? And are you sure suburban moms and urban drag queens wouldn't be interested, too?

Second, identify their life stages. This is where you'll likely find some striking similarities among your segments and even new segments to market to, opening up untapped revenue

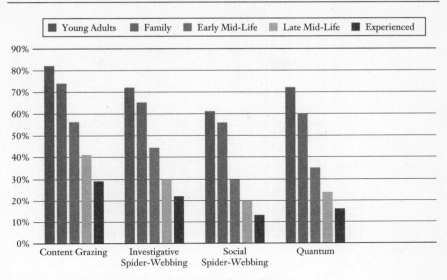

Figure 6.4   Multi-Screen Pathways by Lifestage

streams. Figure 6.4 shows the incidence of the multi-screen pathways we've discussed earlier cut by traditional lifestages: Young Adults, People with Families, Early Mid-Life, Late Mid-Life, and Experienced consumers over 55. When looking at these lifestage demographics, you can see that the incidence of multi-screening behavior declines as age increases.

But let's take a closer look at the "family" demographic set. While financial services has often been thought of as demographic driven—for instance, over-65s have different needs from university kids just signing up for their first checking account—we found some compelling life-stage nuances in our recent Consumer Decision Journey: Financial Services study. The "family" segment actually makes up adults ages 25 to 64— an extremely broad demographic segment. This reality reflects the demographic changes we outlined in the beginning of this chapter. These consumers' needs are less driven by their age and more by the ages of their children. But even then, we see that parents with kids under age 2 span from 25 to 49.

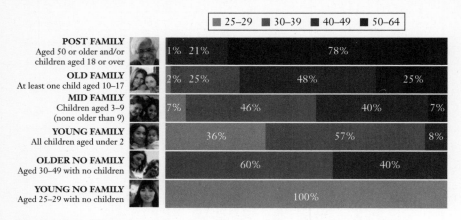

Figure 6.5 The Consumer Decision Journey: Financial Services Lifestage Demographics
Source: The Consumer Decision Journey: Financial Services, Microsoft, and Ipsos OTX, 2014.

If you are a financial services company targeting consumers who want to start saving early for their children's education, for example, you might make the assumption that you should be targeting young parents. But if you targeted only parents ages 25–29, you would miss 65 percent of your audience. Lifestage, therefore, can be more revealing than a date on one's driver's license.

The third step is to identify your target audience's central need as it relates to your product or service. These needs are diverse, but it's important to err on the side of authenticity here. Consumers are more sophisticated than ever before, and when you target specific groups, you want to be sure you're not wasting your marketing dollars being all things to all people. Not dissimilar to our Niche Network recommendations in Chapter 4, you're better off zeroing in on where you can offer real value that aligns to genuine consumer needs. A lot of this means that you need to understand where you're differentiated in the marketplace, but it also means boiling that differentiation down to the emotive payoff for the consumer. That psychedelic nail polish might be the most psychedelic ever, but what's it *really* about? Fun? Identity? Then amplify those consumer needs in your marketing.

This is where the Consumer Decision Journey can really come in handy. If you can target the needs of your consumers at each stage of their journey, you're more likely to move them to the next stage and ultimately meet your marketing goal.

Finally, select the screens and approach that are best fit with the most relevant consumer need and the aligns with your product or service.

What you end up with looks something like this:

Four Steps to the Multi-Screen Demographics That Matter

World Cup Apparel Store Example		
Multi-Screen Incidence	Millennial men and women on mobile phones, tablets while viewing live TV	
Lifestage	Pre-family Young and mid-family	
Consumer Need by Decision Journey Stage	Open to Possibility:	Wanting to arrange a fun viewing of the World Cup with friends; connect with others
	Decision to Buy or Change:	Interacting on social channels and coming into contact with the brand
	Evaluating:	Assessing possible items that remind him/her of the fun of viewing the World Cup while interacting with friends

(*continued*)

Four Steps to the Multi-Screen Demographics That Matter (*continued*)
World Cup Apparel Store Example

	Shopping:	A selection of items that remind him/her of the fun of viewing the World Cup while interacting with friends; a special deal related to the World Cup
	Experiencing:	Wearing the apparel and having positive feelings and memories evoked; brand now top of mind for additional purchases
Brand Alignment	Capture and remember the moment with friends via World Cup apparel	

The end result is that you'll be able to define your optimal audience and catch them in the right mind-set, while making sure you're not missing out on potential sales or wasting your marketing budget by targeting the wrong demographic group.

CASE STUDY: ONE MICROSOFT SEGMENTATION

Microsoft is a big company with a very diverse portfolio. Just a sample: more than 100 million Windows 8 licenses have been sold to date; 250 million plus people have SkyDrive; more than 76 million Xbox 360 consoles have been sold worldwide; Skype users spend up to 2 billion minutes per day using the service; Yammer has over 8 million registered users; Outlook.com has more than 400 million active users; MSN received 5.8 billion page views worldwide in June 2013; and more than 1 billion people around the world use Office.[13]

With such a wide-ranging set of devices and services, coming up with a unified segmentation of Microsoft consumers has not always been easy. That's why it's been more important than ever before for Microsoft to get a deeper understanding of consumers—an understanding that prioritizes their needs and values over classic demographic and behavioral segmentations.

Chloe Fowler, founder of London's Razor Research, uses qualitative techniques to help companies identify segments around consumer values, and helped us developed a unified segmentation strategy in 2011.

"Simply using demographic data to segment customers is a somewhat blunt tool," Fowler said. "It also risks undermining the process in the first place. As different divisions within a business start adopting the segments and then adapting them to reflect the attitudes they think their customers have, the segments can start to take on a life of their own. We notice our clients overlaying their own interpretations of what 'might be' the attitude their segments have toward their brands or their categories and these are often based on their personal knowledge of 1 or 2 people that fit the demographic profile—often from their own private lives!"

Imposing one's personal ideas on a demographic segment is a natural human behavior, but it can lead companies down the wrong path. Value-based or attitudinal philosophies are much more actionable, according to Fowler.

"An attitude or a set of values owned by a member of a particular segment should feel as accurate and credible for a 22-year-old and a 45-year-old, albeit the way they use a particular device or product may be a little different," she said. "We know that they will have very different lifestyles, but if we know they're from the same attitudinal segment, we'll expect that at their core, they share values."

In the fall of 2011, we conducted a two-part segmentation study to understand how—and why—consumers in the United States, U.K., Japan, Germany, and France use the entire suite of Microsoft products; from Windows and Office to the Windows Phone, MSN, Bing, Outlook, and Xbox. Then, we went beyond the numbers to learn about the person behind the segments: Who is she? What does she value? What does she expect from brands? And how does Microsoft enable her daily life? Our goal was to create a more robust, insights-driven narrative that puts a human face on our audience, making it easier for advertisers to tell creative, relevant, and connected stories across platforms.

The initial quantitative portion of the study surveyed Windows operating system users on their usage and attitudes surrounding additional Microsoft products and platforms. Rosetta Research conducted the quantitative study and included data from the United States, U.K., France, Japan, and Germany, with a total sample size of 20,159. Behavioral segments were subsequently created; including: Gamers; Informed and Connected; Efficiency Gurus.

But to really get to know our audience and understand why they were exhibiting these clusters of behaviors, we worked with Fowler and her Razor Research team to conduct in-depth interviews to uncover their motivations, ambitions, and the tools and resources they use to help them achieve their goals. Our approach included one-to-one consumer interviews with representatives of each segment, which took place in U.S. and U.K. homes. As you read through our four segments, you'll notice that the activities each group engages in are relatively similar: they all use e-mail and share on social networks, for example. And while specific segments might skew toward a particular demographic group, each one contains consumers of both genders and a variety of ages and markets. What differentiates them are their values and core needs. As a result, we might reach all of them through MSN, but how we engage them will be different depending on their segment. Below, we've included a summary of our results.

The Productives

Productives are organizers. As a rule, they have their finances and their schedules firmly under control. By being clear on their boundaries, they can easily deal with the challenges that life throws their way. They are not necessarily workaholics—in fact, they are more aware of their work/life balance than most. They value their friends and family, and the tools they use to keep them organized help to ensure this "play" time is protected and maximized. Says one of our Productives: "I like to know what each day will bring and make sure I have time to focus on what matters to me most: friends and family."

Their Passions

- They are passionate about people and experiences.

- They enjoy live events and face-to-face contact.

- They are sports fans—playing and watching—and they live for the moment.

- They enjoy travel and creating their own memories.

How Brands Can Engage Productives

- Keep it simple. Productives are very time-conscious, so don't overwhelm them with nonessential details.

- Save the flash for another segment. Productives don't want to know just what's new—they want to know the clear and simple benefits of things.

- Productives respond to systems and products that feel joined up and cohesive, so it helps if features and benefits are linked.

The Connectors

Connectors love to share their lives with others. Their friends and family are their top priority, and socializing with them—online and face-to-face—is their passion. Connectors need to know what's going on and have a keen interest in local events. They embrace technology and the opportunity it gives to talk to a host of people at once, as well as enabling them to make new friends and share their interests. One of our voracious Connectors says, "There is so much in my world to experience, I want to create memories and share them with others as they unfold."

Their Passions

- Close to home—local is best
- Hobbies that connect them with others
- Communication and connection

How Brands Can Engage Connectors

- Connectors have a bit of a curious streak; celebrity news sites are great places to find them.

- Tell them human stories—benefits demonstrated through real people resonate with Connectors.

- Show them how your brand is connecting intuitively with others. This is especially effective if it's in the moment and has a sense of immediacy and timeliness.

- Where possible, keep your messaging local. Connectors are typically most interested in what's close to home.

- Add small gestures of loyalty such as exclusives, deals, and coupons.

The Media Centrics

Media Centrics have a passion for entertainment. They love stories in all forms: film, music, and games. Their passion is closely related to their sense of identity—they choose their entertainment, tools, and devices carefully, seeing them as a reflection of who they are and what they represent. They rarely follow the herd and consider themselves the center of their own, diverse universe. "I follow my heart and indulge in my passions: music, film/TV, gaming," says a Microsoft Media Centric.

Their Passions

- Subjects where the learning never stops such as film, music, photography—and they stick with them

- Sharing passions with others—but do so gently and when asked

How Brands Can Engage Media Centrics

- Encourage experts and ambassadors to endorse brands and services—a personal connection makes a difference.

- They're competitive—give them opportunities for self-expression and to set themselves apart.

- Demonstrate the benefits of personalized products or hubs.

- Help them find the "*new*" and the "*cool*" without force-feeding them.

- Emphasize product functionality as well as form.

The Mavens

Mavens are super-charged tech users. They are fully switched on to the latest trends and eager to share their discoveries. These are your advocates and influencers—passionate, loud, and opinionated. They hunt out news and information and look beyond the headlines and the buzz to fully understand what new products and services can deliver, and are willing to engage their peers and the experts to take the debates forward. "I love being able to take up and put down hobbies and passions—I like creating memories and skills everywhere," a Microsoft Maven says.

Their Passions

- Never stop learning
- Creating hubs that encapsulate everything they love: equipment for sound, music and gaming, clothes, and cameras
- Love to share expertise with others

How Brands Can Connect to Mavens

- They are self-educators and have a defined world view—they will be reading national and international news and periodicals (online and press).
- Status brands are a keen interest—cars, fashion, beauty/grooming, and audio equipment should all appeal to their sense that they want to maximize experiences with the very best.
- Talk about quality inherent in the functions of products—don't just show them aspirational imagery.
- Use brand ambassadors they respect (e.g., sports stars, intellectuals, business mavericks).

- Encourage them to become brand ambassadors—Mavens are the people that others trust.

These four segments are broad in scope, but differentiated enough to reveal clear differences in the ways you would communicate with one versus another. You may just see elements of your own audience here.

Whether you base your own targeting strategy on predefined segments or not, it is critical that you take the time to know your consumers on a deeper level and not just their vital statistics or behaviors. Otherwise, we'll be hard pressed to keep up with our consumers who are increasingly demanding multi-screen campaigns that are meaningful, relevant, and seamless. The only way we can deliver these campaigns—the right message, in the right moment on the right screen—is by folding needs and motivations into our targeting.

CHAPTER 7

Initiate Action with Seamless Experiences across Screens

HOW TO EXECUTE QUANTUM MULTI-SCREENING FOR YOUR BOTTOM LINE

On a chilly December afternoon in San Francisco, California, Jessica and her sister Brooke are shopping at one of their favorite Hayes Valley boutiques. Jess is looking for new speakers, while Brooke is looking for a unique holiday gift for her boyfriend. They're wearing Nike Fuel Bands and workout gear. Their mobile phones—tricked out with Yelp, Instagram, SnapChat, WhatsApp, and the like—are permanently planted in the palms of their hands. In a span of five minutes, Jess uses her phone to check a price on a Bluetooth speaker system, text a friend about plans to watch the 49ers game the following Sunday, and check times for the latest *Hunger Games* movie, all while maintaining a completely unrelated conversation with her sister as they browse the shelves. In the store, she snaps a quick picture of a speaker system, but she doesn't buy it. Not at that moment.

Brooke uses Uber, a car-service app with geolocation capabilities, to order a car to take them to a movie theater near Union Square. Because their location is known via GPS, Uber can automatically scan for nearby cars; the car arrives in less than five minutes. Brooke's credit card is on file and she's able to rate the driver after they've arrived through the app, keeping the experience seamless and empowering her with the ability to provide real-time feedback. Meanwhile, Jess has purchased tickets on her phone, so they skip the movie line by scanning texted QR codes at the door.

The power shoppers. The ultra-productive. The hyperimpatient. They're often known in our industry as early adopters. Right now, they're more likely to be slightly younger consumers clustered in urban areas with enough disposable income to buy the latest gadgets—the people you consult when you want to buy the hottest Tech Thing for your nephew. But as technology becomes increasingly connected, cheap, and easy to use, before you know it, your elderly neighbor might be using Uber to get to the doctor. Today's early adopters are auguries of tomorrow's status quo. And that's why it's important for marketers to pay attention to them now.

After the movie, Jess will pull up the photo that she took in store and e-mail it to herself. Later, at home on her laptop, she'll pin it to Pinterest and share it with her social networks. She'll research similar products online. And eventually she'll buy it, but from a different store. So while the Hayes Valley retailer was successful in prompting the discovery of a new product, he ultimately didn't seal the deal.

Why? First, he didn't move her along to the next stage of her journey by incrementally adding value on a second screen. It's not enough to provide a great retail experience these days; you have to extend it beyond the store and across screens. Second, he didn't do enough to personalize Jess's experience and help her understand how the product would fit in her life.

So what if the retailer *had* known Jess better? What if he were able to help her visualize how the product might look in her living room, understand how it might sound with her music collection, or learn how to sync it with her fiancé's gaming console? What if he could offer her a completely relevant shopping experience that enabled her to discover, research, and purchase the product seamlessly—from inside the store to her mobile phone to her laptop at home?

Believe it or not, he can. We call it Quantum multi-screening.

QUANTUM MULTI-SCREEN PATHWAYS

In the example above, Jess and Brooke's experience across these screens not only shapes their daily activities, but affects how they make purchase decisions and whether they ultimately buy products and services. In fact, we believe user experience is as important as content: the seamlessness of the experience across screens should guide the way we develop content in a multi-screen world. This has huge implications for marketers who want to provide consumer experiences that drive increased sales.

In Quantum Pathways, the fourth pathway from our Cross-Screen Engagement study, consumers leap over time, space, and screen to achieve a goal. They start an activity on one screen and continue it on another. This pathway is sequential and distinctly intent based; as a result, ease and productivity are paramount. Efficiency is the dominant reason consumers take Quantum pathways, with activities such as working, shopping, and completing tasks coming to the forefront. This is also the pathway consumers are most likely to start at work or on the go. And since we know consumers are increasingly mobile, those interstitial moments in between work and home are now critical touchpoints for marketers who want to keep their customers close and convert consideration to sales.

But while consumers expect consistent, cohesive experiences across screens, technology is often not seamless. Quantum paths can be chaotic and disjointed with clunky workarounds.

Jess had to e-mail herself the picture she took of the speaker to make it easier to open on her computer. What if all her pictures were automatically stored in the Cloud? And what if they could be pulled into a room using virtual reality so Jess could visualize how different products might look in her living room? This capability is here today and becoming more common. Ikea recently included a virtual reality catalog where consumers could scan selected pages and then pull up virtual 3-D images of furniture in their home. Never again will you buy a couch that's too big for your living room.

Marketers should seek out partners who can provide solutions that seed ideas on one screen for further exploration on another. And these solutions should encourage consumers to move to the screen that aligns with core marketing goals. If it's investigation, move her to the computer or tablet. If it's discovery in store, the mobile phone is well placed to capture quick ideas on the go. Says Peter, a U.S. respondent in our Cross-Screen study, "I see stuff when I'm out, like a poster for a concert that I'm interested in. So I'll take a photo of it on my phone and then later at home I'll look into it properly on my laptop." If it's a transaction, computers and increasingly tablets are the place to be. Consumers expect to be able to move from one screen to the next, and marketers have a tremendous opportunity to help smooth the way for them.

As another one of our study respondents said, "The main reason I multi-screen is that I start looking at something on the train or at work and then I need to finish it later. It's efficient. I start my Tesco shopping on the way home from work and then finish it on Sunday from my laptop."[1]

Figure 7.1 shows that most consumers embark on Quantum pathways to be more efficient.

Why do consumers take Quantum multi-screen journeys? Because they have a strong need to be on top of things. Feelings

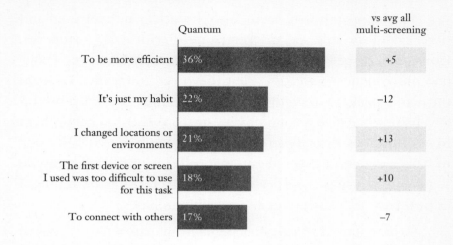

Figure 7.1   Quantum Pathways are about efficiency.

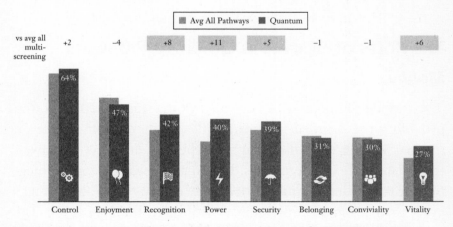

Figure 7.2   Power and recognition are more evident in Quantum Pathways.

of power, recognition, and security are higher with Quantum journeys compared to other multi-screen pathways. Consumers want to feel organized and get things done—and they want to use technology effectively to help them get there. Marketers should seek out opportunities to help consumers feel more efficient through seamless cross-screen experiences, including giving them access to cloud storage, personalization, and rewards for using digital channels (see Figure 7.2).

This approach may seem fairly intuitive, and yet time and time again we still see marketers miss critical opportunities. Consider a diaper company that invites consumers to get a coupon on their next purchase. First they need to locate a code on the diaper package, then they need to type the code into a box on a website to receive a coupon via e-mail. Why not enable them to scan the box directly from their mobile phone via QR code to have a coupon delivered automatically? Eliminating multiple steps and carrying an experience across screens is becoming a critical part of driving sales and repeat purchases.

So how should you approach Quantum pathways in order to increase your bottom line? Here are a few rules of the road based on our research.

THE ROLES OF SCREENS IN QUANTUM PATHWAYS

Mobile

The mobile phone plays a key role in Quantum activities, often providing the original seed of an idea while consumers are on the go. Mobile is used throughout the day, at home and away, to initiate and complete tasks. It's usually used for communication or to dig deeper into something that caught the consumer's eye, giving a sense of immediacy. Mobile technology brings the social, connected component to Quantum activities, often being the hero or ruler of the pathway. This screen is also occasionally used to address decision-making needs on the fly, such as finding movie times or restaurant locations.

TV and Streaming Console

The TV and consoles with video-streaming capabilities are used at home, primarily in the evening when other people are present. They provide content that is often inspirational in nature and frequently the spark for further action. These screens are highly inclusive, their friendly side comes through strongly in our research—remember the Jester and Everyman? They can meet vital discovery and enrichment needs when it comes to decision-making activities.

Laptop or Desktop

Laptops and desktops are used throughout the day in work and home modes. They are the hub for information-gathering and social activities, but also for more involved tasks like video viewing and gaming. Both these screens add greater control to Quantum activities, which is why we still see consumers moving to this screen to conduct deeper research and often for transactions. Laptops and desktops remain key to decision making, particularly information seeking and understanding products and services on a deeper level.

Tablet

The tablet is primarily used at home and provides information and enrichment in a more pleasure-seeking state of mind. It's often used as a discovery tool, but more consumers are also starting to transact on tablets.

In the scenario opening this chapter, Jess needs a seamless experience that takes her from the in-store environment to her home. But, she also wants to visualize how the product fits into her life—that's the personalization need-state in the Consumer Decision Journey that we discussed in Chapter 3. Even as you create marketing campaigns that seamlessly carry consumers across screens, how do you use data to personalize their cross-screen experiences? There are two trends that marketers can now embrace that will enable both seamless and personal experiences across screens; we call them Value Me and the Personal Cloud.

THE CONSUMER-MARKETER VALUE EXCHANGE

Think back to the last decade of consumer technology. In developed markets, we braved inclement weather to stand in line to be the first to get a new model of a mobile phone, scoured the web for sold-out game consoles in time for the holidays (Xbox One: *where are you*?!), and spent hours setting up docking stations and adapters, and running out to Radio Shack for just one more obscure cord that connects X to Y.

In developing worlds, mobile phones opened up a path to engagement for consumers. For many, first-time experiences with the Internet were mobile and distinctly social; apps and social networks *are* the Internet for many consumers around the world—and this had big implications for how consumers used the medium. But wherever you were in the world, we had an almost insatiable hunger for consumer technology.

We've seen a considerable shift in the past few years, indicating a new direction for consumers and their relationships with technology. The financial meltdown of 2008 left governments, economies, and societies looking at the world from a very different perspective. In the Middle East, people were using social media networks to organize dissent. Natural disasters and the evidence of climate change have created a sense of unpredictability. And most recently, the emergence of Edward Snowden has put a face on our evolving notions of personal privacy.

With the economy, climate, politics, culture, and society constantly being reshaped and disrupted, it's only natural that our relationship with technology will also change. Most consumers have now formed long-term relationships with their devices, and as a result, their expectations are different. They want technology that feels more natural in how it helps them address their needs—technology that's not just mobile, but also more personal, responsive, and intuitive.

The Microsoft Digital Trends study we've mentioned throughout the book reveals our maturing relationships with technology. The trend that we're going to focus on in light of Jess's story is what we call Value Me. It's a trend that presents new challenges and opportunities for brands and advertisers of every size. How does that Hayes Valley retailer invite consumers like Jess into experiences—engage and enable them, excite, support, and reward them—in more relevant and human ways? *Valuing consumers* and the data they share with you is a big part of the equation.

Consumers increasingly view their identity as a commodity in the digital space. Their identities have multiple facets, which are becoming heavily managed to enable the exchange of personal data for tangible value. In fact, consumers are starting to see their online identities as marketing profiles with overt value which may even prompt storage of personal data in data vaults with data brokers. We expect to see an increasing need to access these data identities through one simple personal verification system. This system, activated through such personal identifiers as a fingerprint or eye recognition, might just be the new gateway to the digital world.

For each of our future trends, we explored a number of key measures, including the level of awareness or degree of familiarity with each trend, the level of engagement or current involvement with the trend, the level of receptivity for adopting this behavior in the future, as well as the immediate marketing potential of each trend.

For the Value Me trend, 48 percent of the consumers we interviewed know that their data is valuable to marketers.[2] In a short time, more mainstream Internet users will take control of their data and seek reciprocal relationships with brands. Most consumers will demand transparency.

Similarly, 30 percent already know and understand how to exchange data for rewards.[3] Consequently, we expect that online identities will evolve from a collection of behaviors and expressions to becoming more holistic profiles that can be continuously crafted and built upon to gain maximum rewards.

In fact, 59 percent of the consumers we surveyed are interested in selling their data for rewards.[4] Qualitative research with early adopters reveals that they're already thinking about how they can exchange data for something of value. While we don't currently have a global standard of valuation for data, 45 percent of global online consumers say they would be willing to sell all of their digital data collected over a six-month period to the right brand at the right price.[5]

Thirty percent of consumers are aware of the Value Me trend, and they're more likely to use a brand that rewards them for their data.[6] Consumers are not just interested in flat monetary returns, however; they also want better deals for existing experiences. Interestingly, consumers don't think they're getting that value now. As you can see in Figure 7.3, while 66 percent of consumers in our financial services study understand the value of sharing their data to financial services firms, only 31.1 percent are satisfied with what they get in return.[7] As digital relationships mature, consumers are shifting from taking a passive to an active role in creating digital experiences. They are starting to realize the value in their personal data and view it as raw material to building better, more personal experiences. As a result, we'll see consumers starting to take more responsibility for controlling of their data and seeking more reciprocal relationships with brands.

New Behaviors

- Marketing the self for rewards, online and offline
- Data storage services

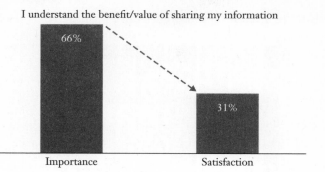

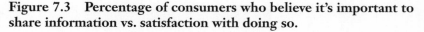

Figure 7.3   Percentage of consumers who believe it's important to share information vs. satisfaction with doing so.

- Personal infographics

- Data bodyguards

- Data inheritance

- Brands investing uniquely in high-value consumers

- Identity verification consolidation

So what can we expect this new world of Value Me to look like (see Figure 7.4)? While many marketers are now beginning to catch on to this trend, it's still not easy to compile consumer data and leverage it in a way that builds more reciprocal consumer-brand relationships. That may soon change, however.

THE PERSONAL CLOUD

Throughout this book, we've repeatedly called out that consumers want more personalized experiences from brands. Even today, it's hard to deny that the most compelling and useful services for consumers are, in fact, highly personalized. These services contain an intimate understanding of the consumer—who they are, what they like, and what they need. And they subsequently leverage this understanding to provide more relevant experiences.

Future Intent to Engage in the "Value Me" Trend

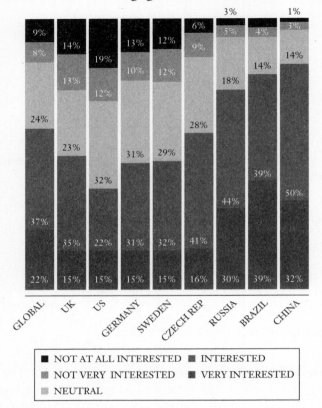

Figure 7.4   Value Me Market Snapshot

The best brands also *anticipate* what the consumer wants, and as a result they're proactive and able to act on behalf of their customers.

Let's take the Uber example from the beginning of this chapter. When I sign up for Uber, I include my name and my payment information. When I need to use it, the app automatically picks up my geolocation. For me, it's often a location in San Francisco, Seattle, Chicago, or Toronto. I don't mind sharing my location at any given time because I know I'm going to get a significant amount of value out of it—the ease of having a car pick me up without having to find the number for a local taxi company and then call them from a noisy office, restaurant, or bar. Because Uber immediately searches for cars in my immediate vicinity, it rarely takes more than five minutes for a car to arrive. And if the driver is at all confused about where to pick me up, he can just text me for clarification. After the car picks me up, I'm able to rate the driver, which not only provides an incentive for drivers to do a good job, it also *involves me* in making Uber a stronger, better service. To me, Uber isn't just a car service, it's a critical part of how I navigate nearly every business trip I take.

You can see the ideas embedded in this example beginning to take shape in many of today's most popular apps. Music applications such as Spotify, Pandora, and Xbox music have become hugely popular by providing personalized radio stations, complete with recommendations based on past preferences. Movie recommendations from Netflix can sometimes reveal more about us than we care to know (my preference for "understated midlife crisis dramas" by the age of 30 was somewhat of a red flag, but what can I say? I love *Wonder Boys*). Personalized news from Zite, restaurant recommendations from OpenTable, Yelp, and UrbanSpoon help us experience, share, and track our preferences.

Almost all of today's big names in technology have made a bet on personalization. Industry analysts from Ericsson predict that there will be 50 *billion* connected devices by the year 2020.[8] Think back to those Nike Fuel Bands Jess and Brooke were wearing in San Francisco. Through these devices and sensors, we'll know just about everything about these shoppers: where they've been, how fast they drive, what they buy, what movies they watch—even the rhythm of their heartbeats.

The proliferation of personal data can lead to both incredible opportunities as well as significant risks. As depicted in the

Uber example, sharing personal data can bring a seamlessness and convenience to our lives that no other generation has enjoyed. Our every desire and need will be predicted and addressed. But this also means that personal privacy as we knew it is quickly becoming a thing of the past. Data security and trust are becoming more important than ever before.

Steve MacBeth, a partner group program manager on Microsoft's engineering team, is currently working on a personalization solution for Microsoft and its partners. MacBeth worked within Microsoft's search team where he focused on increasing the contextual relevance of the algorithm that drives Bing. At the same time, he also wanted to find ways to give marketers more control over their brand within search results. MacBeth's current role is an intersection of these two points: How do you make advertising more personal while giving brands the ability to enter into direct and relevant conversations with consumers?

MacBeth leads a team that is incubating what he calls the Personal Cloud. "The concept of a personal cloud is a way for users to understand and organize all of the data in the digital world around them, and then make that data available to others to deliver better experiences or experiences that contain more value to them," he explains.

The Personal Cloud is owned by the consumer and can be leveraged—with permission—by third parties to provide apps and services across screens. When we talk about creating seamless multi-screen experiences for consumers, it's clear that the Cloud is rapidly becoming a key component; it's often the unifying factor across devices. The Personal Cloud takes it to the next level. In addition to being a developer-oriented platform that allows for data storage, the Personal Cloud is capable of aggregating and exposing personal data stored in other places, essentially bringing in more meaningful and holistic insights that can be shared with brands.

This is important because the way we share consumer data today is both siloed and nontransparent to consumers. "As people, we exist in a coherent way. I see you today and then when I see you later in a different context, you're the same person," he said. "In the digital world, we're highly fragmented beings. Some of it is by choice. I want to show up in gaming in a different context than work. But these boundaries create tiny fragments of users. People end up being represented in fragments: as an Xbox Live user, as a Microsoft Exchange user, as a Bing user—to us, those are all different people. So part of what the personal cloud is trying to do is create a cohesive, more human entity."

Marketers have found ways to create more holistic profiles using cookie exchanges. While many digital marketers use this approach today to track users through browser behavior for targeting, MacBeth contends it doesn't go far enough.

"By putting data into a cookie exchange, I get a more holistic view of the user. This is a solution to the fragmentation problem, but it still lives in the marketer's domain. The Personal Cloud is the inverse of the cookie exchange," MacBeth said. "Rather than give everyone all of the user data, we empower the user to keep the data and simply give permission to certain brands to access it. So on top of aggregating data, we're creating a permissioning system, giving consumers control and a more equitable value exchange as a result."

Our research has shown that when consumers feel in control, they're more likely to share their personal data. In fact, we found in our Consumer Decision Journey Financial Services study that control was the single biggest factor driving consumers to share information: 68 percent are more likely to share their data if they feel in control. Secondarily, they also want the power to stop sharing or delete information at any time.[9]

But is this good for marketers? With consumers' increasing awareness that their data is worth something, marketers need to

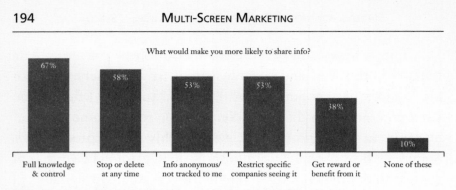

Figure 7.5   **What makes consumers comfortable sharing.**

be prepared to set a higher bar. The Personal Cloud could be the key to fulfilling consumers' expectations for personal experiences with brands, while also building transparent, authentic relationships that yield greater value over the customer lifecycle.

"Marketers benefit by being able to build a real relationship over time with a consumer rather than one with fragmented strands of data," MacBeth said.

Here's an example of how this concept can change the way we market to consumers. MacBeth is a loyal New Balance shoe buyer. Over the past 20 years, he's faithfully purchased a pair of New Balance sneakers just about every two years. But in spite of his loyalty, MacBeth has never seen any indication that New Balance really *knows* him.

"I might be one of their most loyal customers. [The Personal Cloud] would give a company like New Balance the ability to have a digital relationship with me. They would know that fitness is important to me," he said. "If they sent me an e-mail and said, *We've seen the kind of shoe you like; we're going to send a pair of shoes for you to try at 50 percent off. You can send them back if you don't like them*—that would be great. I would love that."

And this gets at MacBeth's core gripe with today's forms of advertising: it's just not helpful. "If I see a New Balance billboard, this doesn't help me at all. Even if I see an ad on the computer, it's not directed enough. Even if I click, I'm still on a generic site. They know nothing about me," MacBeth said. "If they followed up a purchase with a message that said, *Why don't we just do this every two years?* and then signed me up for a subscription to running shoes and shipped me a new pair every two years, I would love that."

(If you're reading, New Balance, call me and I'll send you Steve's address so you can start sending him those running shoes.)

"For companies that can snap to this worldview and add real value, they can get a much broader perspective of the user to understand their preferences, needs, and goals—and then target in a much richer way," MacBeth said. "Rather than focus on creating demand, they can fulfill it in a much more personalized way."

Clearly, this more personal and permissioned relationship opens up new possibilities for brand advocacy, which brings the model full circle. If, as MacBeth says, brands focus more on fulfilling their existing customers' needs in a deeply personal way, then they can focus less on creating demand for new customers—because their current customers will do it for them. As marketers, there's nothing better than having our best customers evangelize our products, but they need to have pretty extraordinary experiences in order to do so. If New Balance made MacBeth's experiences with their brand so personal and so convenient that he grew to have a real relationship with them, a relationship where they really know him, he's much more likely to feel compelled to share his experiences with others. That's consumer-centricity at work.

"I don't believe that being or not being consumer-centric is optional," MacBeth said. "The marketers that make the transition are the ones who will stay in business. It's the same as what happened with e-commerce online. Moving online gave consumers more control—they had information to make more informed choices. But it didn't put them in charge. I think the next step of that evolution will, and it will be just as profound."

CASE STUDY: QUANTUM MULTI-SCREENING + VALUE ME AND THE PERSONAL CLOUD

Let's take a look at what happens when we combine Quantum multi-screening with both the Value Me trend and the Personal Cloud concept. One of MacBeth's key partners at Microsoft is Steven Webster, Senior Director of Experience Design. Webster leads a team of designers and engineers who co-create solutions directly with marketers across Microsoft platforms. From auto-buying experiences to bringing digital meaningfully into a retail journey, Webster's team is adept at creating seamless consumer experiences that add real value to both consumers and marketers.

"Recognizing the need to embrace emerging digital trends and leveraging consumer insights to reveal consumer needs—the why behind their what—is necessary, but not sufficient," Webster said. "We need to continue to keep the consumer at the center when we activate against trends and insights by applying design-thinking."

What is design-led thinking? Webster believes it is the key for creating solutions that are truly consumer-centric.

"Consumer data is the spark for creativity, but creativity relies on design teams that are able to ideate and innovate in the intersections—between user needs, business objectives and a deep understanding of just how far technology can be pushed," he said. "The combination of consumer insight, plus design-led thinking, delivers simple and seemingly magical experiences that move consumers effortlessly across every screen they interact with."

In the interest of showing instead of telling, let's take a look at a prototype Webster's team built based on a consumer scenario that came out of our Auto Consumer Decision Journey research, and guided by the design-led thinking that Webster activates.

Brooke's boyfriend James has downloaded the digital owner's manual that came with his car when he purchased it; it enables him to get data about his car on his tablet, phone,

and laptop, and he stores all his information in the Personal Cloud.

He has complete control over it and is able to choose how, when, where, and with whom he shares it.

One morning, he's working on his Surface when he gets an alert that his car's tire pressure is low. He clicks on the Book Now button so he can schedule an appointment.

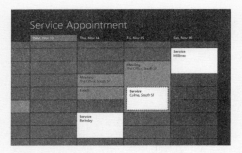

The app is synced up to his outlook calendar and is smart enough to recognize when James has free spots in his schedule. So it suggests a few times when James is not only available, but according to his stored preferences for early mornings or weekends, it also recommends some car service locations based on where James lives, as well as the location of his workplace.

James chooses a time and location that works for him and books his appointment.

He drops off his car, using the mapping service on his phone as his GPS system. He doesn't have to launch the mapping service or program in the location. The phone is "intelligently on"— knowing his appointment time and that he is in his car, it switches automatically to mapping, with a preprogrammed destination.

When he arrives, his phone recognizes that he's there and communicates his arrival to the dealership. A message on his phone subsequently prompts James to drop off his car in Bay 34 and leave his keys in a drop box. A driver employed by the dealership is alerted and drives James back to his office.

Later, James gets an alert on his phone that his car is ready.

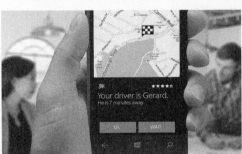

James replies with a time when he will be ready and the dealership lets him know that a driver will be arriving to pick him up at his office.

While James is on the ride back to the dealership to pick up his car, his paperwork is sitting in the passenger seat.

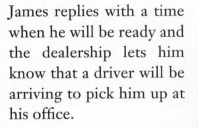

All he has to do is scan it with his mobile phone and sign it.

At home, James gets a message letting him know that his service is complete.

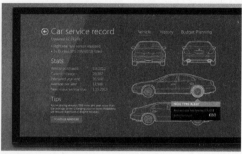

He can pull up additional information about his car and his service record anytime, on any screen. Knowing he hates surprises, the service record warns him of upcoming maintenance, which he can budget and plan for. And the dealership where James had his car fixed can continue its relationship with him, sending relevant messages, recommendations, suggested products, and reminders in a truly personal way.

Anticipatory. Responsive. Natural. Personal. *This* is Quantum Multi-Screening.

IMPLICATIONS FOR MARKETERS

To create truly seamless multi-screen experiences for consumers, there are three critical areas we need to focus on today in order to successfully anticipate tomorrow. As we saw with the Personal Cloud, not all of them have fully arrived on the scene, but we believe that marketers who start creating campaigns with an eye for the future will have a better chance of succeeding.

Marketers should focus first on the sequential or Quantum trend itself: create seamless, friction-free experiences by understanding how each screen can play a role in the consumer's journey and facilitate seamless transitions from screen to screen. They should also relate these back to offline environments like the retail store Jess visited in the opening chapter.

Second, keep the Value Me trend in mind as you leverage data to develop deeper relationships with your customers. Understand that consumers are more willing to give you information than you might think. But like any relationship, it needs to be reciprocal, and it needs to evolve over time. You can imagine the relationship consumers have with your brand and any subsequent data exchange as similar to dating. If you're going out with someone for the first time, you're not going to ask a series of incredibly intrusive personal questions right off the bat. You're going to start with a few basics—name, neighborhood, where they live—and go from there. Over time, you can get more information. That's how you build trust. And if you use that information to foster a reciprocal relationship, it will deepen over time, with consumers feeling that they can trust you to use their data to enhance their experience rather than fear what you might do with it.

Finally, keep a close eye on the development of new ecosystems that enable easier ways to get a holistic view of your customers. This isn't just about a single moment, it's about an ongoing relationship, one where consumers are hyper-aware of the value of their data and how it can earn them more personalized, better brand experiences. If MacBeth is right, the marketers who embrace this new trend—putting consumers in control of their own data and giving brands permission to enter reciprocal relationships with them—will not only increase their bottom line, they might just be the sole survivors of Web 10.0.

CHAPTER 8

Measure Consumer Metrics, Not Device Metrics

AVOID THE DEVICE-FIRST MEASUREMENT TRAP

Our industry is currently faced with significant challenges around how to accurately measure multi-screen campaigns. We find ourselves in the classic chicken-and-egg conundrum: we know we should be developing and deploying multi-screen campaigns to align with consumer behavior, but if we can't measure whether these campaigns drive business results, then how can we justify the investment?

We've made strides in measuring digital advertising, moving from click-through rates to engagement metrics to brand and sales uplift. The next frontier is mobile—do the same metrics apply, or do we need different ways to measure smartphones and tablets? And what about social? Which metrics are meaningful, and how do they sync with digital and mobile metrics? Not only are we struggling to measure impact on newer devices, but connecting them together to assess how a campaign delivers across different screens seems almost insurmountable. We scale one mountain only to see four more peaks on the horizon.

In Chapter 1, we identified three factors underlying many of these measurement challenges: first, the functional complexity of digital devices; second, the legacy of a television-dominated advertising world; and third, the way media is bought and sold. Let's revisit each in turn.

DEVICE COMPLEXITY DRIVES MEASUREMENT COMPLEXITY

It is very easy to get sidetracked from a measurement perspective when focusing on the technological features and functions of each digital device. To begin with, it can be complicated trying to figure out which function to align media against when every device does many different things. For example, a mobile phone can be used for e-mail, texting, search, gaming, and video viewing, so there is a plethora of ways to deploy campaigns on this device: e-mail or texted offers, search, pre-roll videos, and app-based content, to name a few. And each one of these function-focused campaigns will drive a different metric, including redemption, click-through, engagement, recall, brand favorability, and purchase intent. Even if you pinpoint the best mobile metric to evaluate success, you still need to connect it to those generated from your television, computer, or tablet campaign. This problem is especially challenging if you have different campaign objectives for each device, which is not atypical.

We've dealt with this complexity by creating a division of labor for each device: branded emotive advertising for television campaigns, search or pre-roll video for display campaigns on computers, local or tactical offer-based campaigns for mobile, and we're still in the early days with the tablet. Once again, we are back to having separate, very disparate metrics for each individual screen in our campaign. And for many marketers, having a presence on different screens represents a multi-screen campaign. But to truly understand whether your media dollars are well spent, you need to assess the discrete impact of each campaign through media mix modeling (assuming you have data to input into the model) or by measuring each campaign separately and extrapolating the relative success of each device-specific campaign based on disparate metrics. But this is not really multi-screen measurement in a truly integrated sense; we're basically treating each new screen as an incremental media buy (and measuring it accordingly) in the way we considered radio, print, and outdoor incremental to television.

Even if the campaign deploys the same media format across devices—a search campaign on mobile and the computer, or a television campaign and pre-roll video on mobile—we aren't certain whether the metric on one screen is valid or meaningful on another one. We may err on the side of oversimplification with click-through rates or page views, but the risk is that we fail to measure the genuine campaign impact.

On a more sophisticated level, there have been a lot of great initiatives launched to create consistent measures across devices, including digital Gross Rating Points (GRPs), which we'll talk about in more detail shortly. GRPs measure a gross reach figure, for example, 100 GRPs can mean that 100 percent of a marketer's target audience is reached once, or 1 percent of them are reached 100 times, or any combination thereof. Logic suggests that delivering 100 GRPs on primetime TV would yield different results to 100 GRPs in daytime, as would 100 GRPs via radio or 100 GRPs via online pre-roll video. While GRPs give us a common currency across television and digital campaigns, they flag up immediate limitations for campaigns that deploy multiple media formats across screens. It's no wonder we default to focusing on each device in isolation rather than truly deploying integrated multi-screen marketing campaigns.

THE LEGACY OF TELEVISION

Television is our legacy screen—it has dominated advertising since the Mad Men of the 1960s started to see the power and potential of sight, sound, and motion. Not only was there far more creative potential on television than through static advertising channels like print, billboard, or audio-dependent radio, but advertisers suddenly had the ability to be in people's living rooms, where their audience sat rapt with attention every night eating their TV dinners and watching variety shows.

Given the centrality of television advertising both for marketers and consumers alike, it is not surprising that the large shadow of this screen continues to loom across the media industry. It remains a powerful vehicle for reaching broad audiences; still provides a great conduit for emotive, brand-focused advertising; and, most important, it's measurable thanks to Nielsen, who pioneered the set-top box and the world of ratings and reach.

But even for TV, GRPs can be flawed. Marketers are trying to reach niche audiences via TV may struggle with the reliability of small panel sizes. And just measuring reach and frequency is not enough, even for TV. As an industry, we have accepted these limitations and have folded in supplementary measurement tools, like brand tracker surveys, to get a more holistic view of campaign performance.

There has been a natural tendency in the multi-screen world to take what is familiar—TV GRPs—and apply it to the rest of the media ecosystem. We observe this across the board—if you have a great television ad, then it's tempting to stream it on mobiles, tablets, and PCs. And similarly, if we have a robust system for measuring the success of television advertising, then let's take those tried-and-true metrics and apply them to other, newer screens. The instinct to work with what we have (and what delivers) hasn't been misguided—it has at least given us a starting point as we tackle the complexity of measuring media impact on single devices and across screens. But we need to be careful that we don't make overarching assumptions that consumers respond to each screen in the same way—and that their motivations for using each screen are the same. We know from our research that consumers relate very differently to each screen—remember the mobile as the Lover?—and use screens very differently depending on their needs and motivations. The point here is to not introduce complexity. We are united in our desire to have a valid, robust, and meaningful system for measuring multi-screen campaigns. But we also want to make sure that in our drive to simplify, we don't become reductionist and end up applying metrics that are inadequate, not relevant, or even worse—measure the wrong thing.

Let's take a deeper look at what we consider legacy metrics, which fall into three buckets: GRP, brand, and sales.

Gross Ratings Points

GRPs are the standard currency for measuring traditional media—but were primarily developed to measure the effectiveness of television campaigns. As a refresher, GRPs measure two things: whether the right audience was "reached" by the campaign and how frequently the campaign was viewed. The official formula is:

$$\text{GRP} = \%\text{ audience reach (000s divided by audience universe} \times 100) \times \text{frequency (average exposure per person)}$$

At the end of the day, GRPs are a pretty blunt measure considering all the ways we could look at human behavior, but if your objective is mass reach and exposure, you will at least know whether a critical number of people saw your campaign.

Generally, most marketers will want more versus fewer people to see their campaign, and it is also critical that the *right* people see your campaign. So, reach is also about optimizing exposure among your target audience: moms, teenage boys, men between the ages of 25 and 45. In Chapter 6, we focus on the evolving nature of targeting and make a case for moving beyond demographic and behavioral targeting to defining audience on the basis of needs and motivations. But, in theory, a more finite and sophisticated approach to targeting doesn't compromise the overarching validity of GRPs—it just means we are aiming to get more precision around reach to ensure we get our campaigns in front of the most relevant and positively predisposed audience.

There has been ongoing debate over the years around the value of "exposure" as a measure of campaign success. How many times do you really want someone to see your campaign? Some marketers adhere to the notion of *"recency,"* which is based on the theory that if your campaign doesn't shift perceptions or drive behavior the first time it's viewed, you aren't going to get much more leverage the third, fourth, or fifth time people see your ad. Whether you buy into this notion or not when it comes to television advertising, recency is embedded into how we think about delivering campaigns in the digital and multi-screen world.

With television, there are a lot of contingencies that make recency a bit challenging. You need to count on the fact that people didn't fast forward through your ad or go to the fridge for some ice cream during the commercial break. With digital, we aspire to target and message people at the right moment on the right screen, and increasingly, we want technology that enables this level of precision. Given this, the notion of "exposure" becomes far more nuanced in the digital space. Do we really aspire to have consumers see our campaign five times? Or would we rather that they see it once, in the moment when they are most receptive to the message and most likely to act on it?

Conceptually, we need to adjust how we think about GRPs in the multi-screen world. If our objective with multi-screen marketing is to deliver meaningful, additive advertising experiences on the right screen in the right moment, we need to recalibrate to focus on quality as much as quantity. "Reach" is not just about numbers (quantity), it's also about targeting the most relevant audience (quality) at scale. "Exposure" is not just about optimizing the number of times people see our campaign (quantity), but also about ensuring they see it at the right moment when they want and need the information we are conveying (quality). If we're not starting to think more about quality over quantity in the way we measure the success of multi-screen campaigns, we may be exerting a lot of technical energy on imprecise measures.

To be clear, we are not even going to begin detailing the engineering and mathematical challenges of creating a standardized GRP measure that can assess reach across television, the computer, and mobile devices. Nielsen, ComScore, and others have been taking on this challenge, and there is virtue in pursuing a multi-screen GRP metric if it provides us with a common currency for assessing media performance across multiple devices. What we want to raise for consideration is whether we refine and rethink the building blocks of GRPs to ensure that the uber-metric we ultimately land on aligns with the caliber of campaigns that we aspire to deliver to consumers across screens.

Brand Metrics

When evaluating traditional media, brand metrics are often used in conjunction with GRPs to provide a more nuanced read on ad performance. While GRPs deliver a macro view on whether the right number of people saw a campaign, brand metrics evaluate whether the campaign, including both creative content and media placement, are shifting perceptions of the brand in the right direction. This approach has been co-opted with reasonable success into the world of digital advertising, with the following set of measures typically making an appearance:

- Unprompted and prompted awareness of the advertisement

- Unprompted and prompted awareness of the brand and product in the advertisement

- Positive or negative associations with the advertising

- Brand perceptions (usually anchored in specific brand characteristics the advertiser seeks to emphasize or shift)

- Purchase consideration or intent

Typically, these metrics are captured through direct-to-consumer surveys that are given to people who have seen the campaign ("exposed") and those who haven't ("control"). Many of you have probably conducted hundreds of these brand metric studies over the course of your careers. We all agree that these studies are not definitive reads on a campaign's success, but they at least provide a high-level view on whether the campaign is having a positive impact.

In the multi-screen world, these studies are not terribly complicated to execute, particularly when focused on established screens like the computer and, increasingly, the mobile phone. The real executional challenges become more acute when you try to measure the aggregate impact of a multi-screen campaign. The obstacle to date has been the ability to track a single consumer across all screens. Without this capability, it is nearly impossible to assess whether the "exposed" group viewed the entire campaign across each screen. As a result, what is straightforward to execute on a single screen becomes more difficult with each additional screen that's folded into the campaign mix. Further, we need to think about whether these measures are adequate if our objective is to create truly seamless cross-screen advertising experiences. This isn't to say that we don't want to validate that people see our advertising and respond positively to it, but that we should also determine whether we need to include new measures into the mix that are not just focused on marketer KPIs.

Sales Metrics

Sales metrics are the "holy grail" of campaign measurement. It's great to know that we've shifted brand consideration and that people like our ad—but at the end of the day, most of the advertising we do is meant to drive sales. Measuring actual sales (versus purchase intent or consideration) that we can attribute directly to advertising has been a longstanding challenge in the world of traditional media and brick and mortar retail. In the world of digital retail, connecting advertising to digital sales is much easier—we can track an initial click-through to an online purchase. However, the majority of sales still occur offline, so we continue to contend with the complications of linking advertising exposure to these offline purchases.

Observing an uptick in sales following the run of an advertising campaign doesn't give us the ammunition we need to prove that the campaign was singularly responsible for driving people to purchase. If, during the campaign period, everything remained constant except for our one big television campaign, it might be safe to attribute sales to advertising, but the world doesn't stand still when we advertise. To begin with, most campaigns—even in the world of traditional media—usually ignite multiple channels, including print, radio, in-store activity such as promotions or coupons, and even public relations. Then, you need to factor in more intangible factors that can influence sales: the health of the economy, weather patterns, competitor activity, word of mouth, product placement on the shelf, and the list goes on.

Even in a simpler world, attributing sales solely to campaign activity is a tricky business. But companies like Nielsen, ComScore, and IRI, who use a variety of methodologies to collect sales data all the way down to the individual product (SKU) level, are helping us get better at estimating marketing return on investment (ROI). This data is fed into Marketing or Media Mix Modeling that enables us to disentangle the individual effects of what is driving product sales. And, critically, these models help us isolate factors that are beyond our control, such as the weather or macroeconomic conditions, in order to get a purer read on the impact of individual media campaigns on different platforms. While this sounds like a nirvana of sorts—and as modeling gets more and more sophisticated, these models are often our best bets—they are still only as good as the data that we plug into them.

Sales and spend data are fairly easy to acquire and input, but the obstacle can be getting reliable data on platforms other than television. Certain media channels have been notoriously difficult to measure: PR, even radio. And when we start to thrust these models into the multi-screen measurement world, the data challenges become more acute. If PR is hard to measure and input, how do you manage Social, particularly if the campaign is relatively small scale? We are getting better at inputting data from bigger digital campaigns (both search and video based), but now we have to contend with how to get valid, variable campaign data from mobile and tablets.

Even though our modeling capabilities are improving, we are still stymied when it comes to getting the data we need to model the impact of multi-screen campaigns. If we can sort out the data-input issue, Marketing and Media Mix Modeling still represent the best hope we have to truly assess the impact of each individual screen in isolation, as well as multi-screen campaigns in aggregate. But getting the data inputs right is not going to happen overnight. And for many smaller companies, Marketing or Media Mix Modeling is not even in the cards given the scope of their marketing spend or activities. So we need to get creative about how to measure multi-screen campaigns while we sort out the data issues around new platforms and try to find measurement solutions that work for smaller scale campaigns.

MEDIA BUYING, PLANNING, AND CONTENT

The third factor complicating cross-screen measurement is the silos around media planning and buying on both the agency and marketer sides. This is starting to change as the challenges of disaggregated media planning and buying drives restructuring at agencies, but there is still a legacy of media being bought in a non-integrated way.

Marketers may even have specialized agencies managing their traditional, digital, and social campaigns, a solution that provides high levels of expertise but considerable fragmentation. Any degree of fragmentation in media buys across screens makes true multi-screen measurement very challenging. Not only do you have separate groups specializing in specific media channels— television, digital and mobile, gaming, social—but each is going to be focused on maximizing campaign results on its individual platforms. As a result, integrated measurement is not really prioritized and may even be opposed to the interests of each planning and buying group.

This problem can be even more pronounced if there are separate agencies planning and buying media across different platforms. Each agency has a strong incentive to demonstrate the efficacy of its discrete media buys in order to retain business and increase spend. The only way that true multi-screen measurement can occur—and this presupposes that there is an integrated campaign to begin with—is when you default to media mix modeling, dependent upon getting data by platform. If not, you have each publisher or platform provider delivering their own campaign effectiveness studies that often equate to a lot of drops of water that add up to only a half-full glass. You can get a reasonable read of whether your banner ad, television campaign, video pre-roll, and social campaign delivered against broad-based objectives (usually brand), but it is pretty challenging to extrapolate which of these individual efforts was more or less successful. Which should be retained, ramped up, or dumped? The burden usually falls on the primary media planning agency or the internal media measurement teams on the marketer side to make this assessment, and it is by no means a straightforward task, particularly with CMOs and CFOs scrutinizing every dollar, euro, or pound invested in marketing efforts.

Things get even more complicated when you fold in the creative content—the actual substance of the campaign that appears on the different screens. In the media world, we have a terrible tendency to attribute the success or failure of a campaign to the screen or channel on which it appears. It's not that we discount the importance of creative content, but that responsibility belongs to the bearded guys with the dark-framed glasses and hip ladies in skinny jeans sitting over at the creative agency. And while we're feverishly figuring out which screen or combination of screens to include in the campaign, our skinny-jeaned friends are testing creative ideas, messaging, script vetting, and copy testing their creative to make sure it resonates with consumers. Both groups are working on optimizing their piece of the puzzle.

As discussed in Chapter 2, it is not always the case that creative is developed to correspond with the distinct relationship consumers have with each screen or even optimized for different screens. Ultimately, if the creative is a miss, it could be on the biggest billboard in the world but not drive positive impact for a product or brand. Developing the right creative content for the right screen—which is critically important—adds layers of complexity from both a planning and measurement perspective. How do we measure the discrete impact of the creative, the channel, and whether the content and channel are working well together? Most of the metrics we currently employ in our screen-by-screen campaign assessments don't always pull apart the impact of the creative over that of the media channel. And when you think about the spirit of a true, integrated multi-screen campaign, you really shouldn't pull the two apart. Consumers aren't thinking, *"Wow, that was a brilliant advertising campaign—such emotionally powerful creative! And, I'm so glad it was on my mobile phone and not my television—I really feel more connected to the brand now that I've seen this campaign on my phone."* Consumers are focused on the content first and foremost; they probably only think about the device serving up the content if the overall experience is unpleasantly disruptive, incongruent, or irritating.

As discussed in the previous chapter, consumers want and expect a seamless content experience across screens—it should feel natural, relevant, and joined up, almost as though they aren't being advertised to at all. At the heart of delivering these experiences is understanding the specific need or motivation that consumers are seeking to address as they engage with content across screens. If we identify these underlying needs, we can begin to deploy the right content on each screen and get more clarity around what we should be measuring. We believe reframing what we're actually trying to measure will lead to a simplified, more accurate and meaningful set of metrics for multi-screen measurement. At the heart of this effort is shifting from a platform-centric approach toward a content-focused, consumer-centric orientation.

CONSUMER-CENTRIC MULTI-SCREEN MEASUREMENT

A consumer-centric approach to measurement does not mean that we subvert marketing objectives or stop caring about whether multi-screen campaigns deliver against broader business goals. What we are suggesting instead is that we move away from a platform-focused, marketing-centric approach to measurement— reach, exposure, awareness, purchase consideration by device—to one that aligns marketer objectives with consumer needs.

To truly deliver seamless, consumer-centric multi-screen campaigns that align with consumer needs, we need to start evaluating whether our campaigns are actually delivering value to consumers. When our campaign objectives are exclusively marketer focused—we want to build awareness through mass reach, cultivate brand loyalty, drive purchases—the metrics we use to measure whether the campaign is successful will align with our goals as marketers. And, naturally, we will build campaigns and media plans that have the highest probability of delivering against these marketer-focused metrics. But the real risk here is that we lose touch with what consumers are seeking because the entire system we have in place to build and measure campaigns is all about us and not about the consumer, the very person we're trying to influence in the first place.

As we've discussed throughout this book, when we veer off the path of being grounded in a consumer-centric orientation focused on consumer needs and motivations, we make building, deploying, and measuring multi-screen campaigns needlessly complex. Focusing on device functions and features, figuring out which marketer-focused metrics can best be delivered by which screen, and trying to navigate through mountains of disconnected data streams will only keep us from delivering the seamless multi-screen campaigns consumers want and expect.

What we measure dictates what we build. So how do we identify meaningful consumer metrics that not only align with marketer objectives, but also simplify how we assess the performance of multi-screen campaigns?

One of the frameworks that we've introduced in this book is particularly well suited to shedding some light here: the Consumer Decision Journey (CDJ). The CDJ framework is by definition consumer centric. Each of the five steps that anchor the framework is defined by the specific decisions consumers make along the path to purchase. At each stage in the journey, we can identify consumers' content needs and which screens they turn to in order to get these needs addressed. Critically, each of these five decision stages very clearly maps to traditional marketer objectives. Once we are clear which consumer decisions we want to influence—likely driven by which ones align with our marketing and business objectives—we can identify which content needs to focus on and what screens to deploy. And, we start to get clarity on what we should be measuring from a consumer perspective: Did our campaign and media plan address consumers' content needs and help them reach a decision? Then, we can fold in our marketer metrics: Did the campaign also deliver against awareness, advocacy, or sales? While the CDJ is not the only, definitive route to identifying measures that will transform multi-screen measurement and elevate cross-platform campaigns, we do think it's an important starting point. Let's explore in more depth why we think this is the case.

By now, you are probably familiar with each of the five decision-making steps in the CDJ: Open to Possibility, Decision to Buy or Change, Evaluating, Shopping, and Experiencing. Before we go too deep into how the framework can be used to generate consumer metrics, let's do a quick refresh on each decision stage (please feel free to skip if you are now a bona fide expert!).

1. Open to Possibility: the confluence of information, marketing content, and interactions with others driving receptivity to a new product/brand/service

2. Decision to Buy or Change: identifying a set of product features and benefits that address needs better than the current product/brand/service

3. Evaluating: identifying which brands or manufacturers best deliver against the desired product features and benefits

4. Shopping: finding and buying the branded product or service

5. Experiencing: trying the product and confirming that it delivers against promised features and benefits and having other people validate that the purchase decision was the right one

As the table below illustrates, each one of these consumer decision stages is tightly aligned with marketer objectives:

Open to Possibility	Decision to Buy or Change	Evaluating	Shopping	Experiencing
Penetration Awareness: Product/ Brand	Consideration: Product Features/ Benefits	Consideration: Brand Benefit/ Product Benefit	Conversion	Advocacy/ Loyalty/Repeat Purchase

So, how do you begin to build and measure a campaign using the CDJ framework? As a starting point, marketers need to identify which phases of the CDJ correspond with their business objectives. If, for example, you are trying to get new consumers to use your product or brand, then your campaign will concentrate on the three early stages of the Consumer Decision Journey: Open to Possibility, Decision to Buy or Change, and Evaluating.

The second step is to identify the core needs consumers have at each of these three stages to inform content for the campaign. As discussed in Chapter 3, consumer needs will vary by vertical, and we encourage you to refer to this chapter for explicit guidelines for your business on the content needs for each decision-making stage. For the sake of illustration, let's say that three overarching needs are identified:

1. Personalization: How does this product or brand fit into my life? (Open to Possibility stage)

2. Information: What specific features, benefits and attributes does this product have? (Decision to Buy or Change stage)

3. Enrichment: Does a brand's emotional promise align with the desired product features and benefits? (Evaluating stage)

The third step is to identify which screens to deploy in your campaign. We know that consumers will turn to specific screens at each of the three decision-making stages in order to meet their content needs. For our example, we'll say that for the Open to Possibility stage, where consumers have personalization needs, they are most influenced by expert blogs and niche networks that they access on their mobiles; in the Decision to Buy or Change stage, to get their informational needs met, consumers rely on branded websites that they view on their computers and tablets; finally, in the Evaluating stage, when consumers want to be inspired by what a brand can deliver, rich media videos viewed on tablets and computers come to the fore.

Now, the pieces of our campaign are coming together. Not only are we clear on how each phase of the decision journey aligns to our marketer objectives, we now have three specific consumer inputs that we can start to operationalize as metrics:

1. Consumer Decision Phase: Did consumers successfully make a decision at each relevant phase?

2. Consumer Needs: Did the content we deliver address their needs and facilitate a decision?

3. The "Right" Screen: Did consumers access this content on the relevant (to them) screen?

Now we can start to bottom out our consumer metrics. As a key starting point, we would argue that the second metric—content that aligns with consumer needs—is the most critical. And, given that the notion that "Content is King" is increasingly invoked in the media world, there is likely to be broad agreement that we need to develop better measures around the content each screen is enabling. Otherwise, we will struggle to deploy campaigns that deliver seamless multi-screen experiences.

Now, our multi-screen measurement system starts to take shape:

Decision Phase:	Open to Possibility	Decision to Buy or Change	Evaluating
Marketer Metrics	*Penetration:* % of new consumers buying *Awareness*	*Awareness:* Product Features/ Benefits	*Consideration:* Brand Benefit/ Product Benefit
Consumer Needs Based Metrics	*Personalization:* Compared to what you currently buy, how well do you think product X fits into your life (better, the same, worse)?	*Information:* How important to you are the following features/ benefits?	*Enrichment:* Which brand best delivers the following features/ benefits?
Consumer Decision Based Metrics	Are you considering changing your current product/ willing to try something new?	Is there a product that you are considering that fits with X set of benefits?	Is there a brand that you are considering that best fits what you are looking for in product X?

The consumer metrics themselves are not revolutionary—they are simple, consumer-centric questions that can be served up in much the same way we ask questions formulated to assess traditional marketer metrics, such as awareness, likeability, or purchase intent. But conceptually, they take us in a new direction and enable us to understand whether the content we're serving up on the relevant screen is facilitating consumer needs and driving each decision-making step in alignment with our marketer goals.

What is equally critical is that we serve up these questions on the right screen in the right moment—otherwise, we can't really assess whether the content and screen are working synergistically to address consumer needs.

One approach that begins to integrate consumer-centric metrics is a tool we're experimenting with at Microsoft called the CDJ Measurement Tool. We'll discuss how this tool works conceptually in the next section. But there are other, more immediate ways of collecting consumer key performance indicators (KPIs) in the moments that matter.

Shelley Zalis of IPSOS-OTX has built a way to deliver consumer metrics in a contextually meaningful way. Her starting assumption—assertion even—is that if we want to successfully measure the impact of multi-screen campaigns, we need to shift our focus from media measurement to content evaluation. We agree—and here's why.

Consumers turn to screens to access content that helps them meet their needs, whether informational, investigative, task-oriented, entertaining, or leisure-oriented.

"We need to focus on in-the-moment measurement tools that help us assess whether we are delivering content when consumers want and need it," Zalis says. "In today's digital world, we have the technology to measure content in real time. Collecting data after the fact won't help us evaluate whether content is really delivering against people's needs, on the right screen and in the moment that matters."

Using the technology that Shelley and her team have developed, it is possible to tag relevant content in real time and collect consumer-driven KPIs, including whether content has addressed specific needs flagged up by the Consumer Decision Journey and supported decision making.

The key point is that focusing on measuring whether or not content is addressing core consumer needs—the basis of consumer-driven metrics—is a powerful framework for measuring multi-screen campaigns. Taking a consumer-centric orientation introduces clarity and simplicity and is organically multi-screen, since consumers naturally gravitate to different screens to get the content they need. This approach is additive to our current efforts in the industry to track consumers as they journey across screens. Now, let's turn to the Consumer Decision Journey Measurement Tool that we're incubating at Microsoft.

A NEW APPROACH: THE CDJ MEASUREMENT TOOL

As we roll out the Consumer Decision Journey to our customers as a framework for consumer-centric content and media planning, we inevitably get asked to "prove out" that this model works in practice and isn't just conceptually useful. In response, we're working on integrating the CDJ framework into a tool to help marketers plan, optimize and measure consumer-anchored multi-screen campaigns. We need to be clear at the outset—we are still in the construction phase of an early pilot of the tool, working with one of our agency partners.

Our "north star" for the CDJ Measurement Tool is to create a system distinctly anchored in a consumer-centric orientation that measures both integrated media plans, while also identifying and measuring the underlying insights needed to create effective messaging. Note that this tool is being built across different verticals since needs and media influencers vary depending on what people are actually buying. As a starting point, the tool is focused primarily on helping customers plan and build a multi-screen campaign—and then measure its success in-flight and post campaign. The development plan has three phases:

1. Phase One: Content Planning/Visualization
   - Identify and align consumer needs and marketer objectives at each stage in the journey to inform content planning.
   - Develop an integrated multi-screen media plan that identifies the optimal screens at each journey stage to address content needs and facilitate purchase decision making.

2. Phase Two: Optimization Tool
   - Use the power of Microsoft's first- and third-party data to pre-optimize the integrated plan from Phase One using both machine learning and predictive analytics.
   - Add other media vehicles into the optimization tool and provide a link back to planner's software tools.
   - Optimize during the campaign based on customer's objectives.

3. Phase Three: Measurement Tool
   - Post-campaign measurement based on integrated internal and third-party data that uses both consumer metrics (content delivers against needs) and marketer metrics (brand, sales).

Our objective in sharing the CDJ Measurement Tool is not to tease people with a blueprint that hasn't been built and then leave everyone hanging. Rather, we want to demonstrate that it is critical to start thinking differently about measurement in the multi-screen world and to assure marketers that there are many ways to skin this cat. But first and foremost, we need to move away from a media measurement focus that is grounded on devices and traditional metrics that are not optimized for a multi-screen world. We need to start to think like our consumers who have already moved beyond screens and are focused on getting the content they need on the screen that they use most naturally.

MARKETER IMPLICATIONS

The CDJ Measurement Tool is certainly one way to isolate meaningful consumer KPIs that can help us develop and measure multi-screen campaigns, but we encourage marketers to experiment with additional ideas in order to move the industry forward. There are three core ways to start adjusting the way we measure multi-screen advertising in order to shift to a consumer-centric perspective:

1. Focus on content over media.

2. Create content that supports consumer needs at each stage in their journey, deployed on the relevant screen.

3. Build metrics that align the consumer need with marketer objectives.

If we don't focus on how effective our content is in supporting consumer decision-making needs, we will continue to build campaigns that fall short of the integrated multi-screen experiences consumers expect and want. The more we hang onto the legacy of marketer-focused metrics, the further behind we'll fall and the more spurious, disconnected, and irrelevant our advertising will become. We need to run apace with consumers who have already moved beyond a screen orientation and are simply getting content where and when they need it to make their lives more streamlined, simple, and stress free.

CHAPTER 9

Meet Your Customer in Her Moment

If we were to cut to the chase and lay out the one primary theme in this book, it would be pretty simple: keep your customer central to your multi-screen marketing strategy. And while that high-level insight might seem intuitive, as marketers, most of us are still pressured to take a line-item approach to marketing—mobile, social, display, traditional—rather than starting with our customer's needs and using them as the foundation for a multi-screen strategy. Putting yourself in the shoes of your customer is a good start; but, now, we also have to surround ourselves with her devices, too. Would you want to be inundated with mobile advertising when you're running late to pick up your kids and trying to find the address of a play date in your phone? Probably not.

In the first chapter, we described a typical day with Stacy, a busy professional mom, and Jen, a small boutique clothing owner. Let's revisit both, but this time, let's work within an ideal multi-screen scenario.

Stacy needs a few items for the fall season. She's been to Jen's boutique before, but it may not be top of mind for her, so like many retailers, Jen sends Stacy a special fall deal to get her in the store. While this is not revolutionary in and of itself, Jen knows that if Stacy is like many of her customers, her mobile phone is how she keeps it all together—her assistant, alarm clock, mapping system, camera, and life enabler—so rather than sending the offer via mail, Jen uses e-mail. She makes sure to emphasize that the percentage coupon can be used in store or on Jen's website with a simple personalized code. Then, she takes it a step further.

She keeps careful records of what her customers have bought in the past and has hired someone to set up an easy algorithm that pulls similar items into the e-mail offer. It also weaves in top-selling clothes that align with customers' past purchases. So, when Stacy gets the offer in her inbox, she sees two sweaters similar to one she purchased before as well as a pair of pants to match. These inspire her Open to Possibility moment; now, Jen's store is top of mind for her fall shopping trip. The call to action on the e-mail tells Stacy that she can fill her cart online, and then schedule time to come into the store to try those items on. Later that night, Stacy goes shopping at her dining room table after the kids have gone to bed.

Meanwhile, when Jen gets to the store in the morning, she sees that Stacy has scheduled some time on Saturday to come in to try on the two sweaters, plus a blouse that has caught her eye on Jen's website. Jen pulls these items in Stacy's size and adds a belt and a skirt she thinks would look nice. She sets them aside to have them ready for Stacy when she comes in.

On Saturday, Stacy has only 40 minutes to run into the store before her son's soccer game, so while she's delighted by Jen's curated selection, she only has time to try on a few of the items. She's unsure about the skirt—it may not be her color—so she snaps a picture of herself in the dressing room mirror and sends it to a friend to get a second opinion. Then, she makes her purchases and rushes out the door.

In the meantime, Jen adds what's left to Stacy's Virtual Wardrobe so Stacy can explore these looks from home on her tablet, whenever it suits her. Later in the week, Stacy is viewing these items while watching television and gets a prompt to update her profile. Since she's had such a positive experience, she fills in a few short questions, letting Jen know a bit more about her: some upcoming special occasions, her favorite designer, and where she and her husband like to go on vacation. As you can imagine, Jen can use this information to send Stacy offers before she leaves for trips, find dresses in her size before special occasions, and let her know about new arrivals.

In fact, over the course of the next six months, Stacy continues to pop into Jen's store and visit her website, building a deeper relationship as she shares more information about her preferences, while Jen layers in even more personalized services, leveraging each screen to add incremental value: the mobile phone for offers and timely alerts, the computer for campaigns that showcase the origin of Jen's boutique, and the designers who make the clothes, and the tablet for more relaxed exploration. Ultimately, Stacy's Experiencing stage becomes her social networks' Open to Possibility moment as she starts to advocate for Jen's services to new customers.

As you can see from the example above, the techniques we use to reach and engage customers aren't necessarily different at the core—it's still about content that meets the needs of your customers—but they are distributed in fundamentally new ways. Advertising has been around for a long time. And while the Internet may have changed the way we do it, the truth is, people really haven't changed much. It's true that their relationships with technology are evolving, as we saw in Chapter 7, and their expectations are increasing. People are starting to see their devices as enabling and amplifying their lives, rather than as separate entities that distract them from living. As Rick Chavez, Chief Solutions Officer at Microsoft is fond of saying, "Consumers expect digital to wrap around their lives."

But so far, our methods aren't working. We're not wrapping around consumers' lives, we've asked them to wrap around our marketing objectives. After all, as we've asserted several times in this book, multi-screen marketing does not mean executing a campaign on every screen; it means creating the right campaign on the right screen at the right time. When content flows across screens, it needs to connect with the core needs of your customer in order to provide them with a truly seamless and valuable experience.

We will be the first to admit that we don't have all the answers—and in fact, one of the reasons we love being in this business right now is that's it's such a dynamic time. But our aim in writing this book is to shed light on how marketers can simplify an incredibly complex new marketing challenge, no matter what new form factor may come our way tomorrow, by staying laser-focused on the needs of their customers. When our industry's focus shifts from tablets, mobile phones, and computers to the consumers who are using them, we uncover meaningful patterns of consumer motivation. A deep understanding of these patterns enables business professionals, designers, and technologists to leverage the right screen with the right message in the right moment—subsequently bringing true utility to consumers and, in turn, deeper value for marketers.

In summary, here are the seven things you need to know to reach your customers across televisions, computers, tablets and mobile phones.

1. *Meet the People behind the Screens*

    Leverage archetypes to help you understand the relationships consumers have with each screen. The TV is the Jester and Everyman, the computer is the Sage, the tablet is the Explorer, and the mobile phone is the Lover. Focus on the screen that best fits your business objectives, as Yezi Tea did when it decided to embark on an education campaign deployed on the Sage (or computer) in Chapter 2.

2. *Understand Your Customers' Decision Journey*

Leverage this five-stage framework to illuminate how consumers make decisions along their paths to purchase. Layer in what you know about your customers and then align your marketing to the influences and needs that come to the forefront at each decision-making stage: the influencers guide which screen to deploy, and the needs shed light on the content consumers seek to make their purchase decisions easier and better.

3. *Introducing Quality Social*

Don't get distracted by social media line items; instead, leverage social as a fundamental human need rather than as a platform. Understand the passion points of your customers, as the La Marzocco case study demonstrated, and enter into authentic conversations within niche networks—that's the power of Quality Social.

4. *Simplify Your Multi-Screen Content Strategy*

Rather than throw everything and the kitchen sink into your content strategy, start curating content for your customers. Give them options—but not too many. And then validate their choices, as VW did through innovative social campaigns that make your customers part of the story.

5. *Drive Efficiency by Targeting Consumer Needs, Not "Millennials and Moms"*

While we've come a long way from demographic to behavioral targeting online, we need to shift to even smarter targeting, where consumer lifestages and values are taken into account. Focus on your customers' core needs to ensure you deliver the right content on the optimal screen in the moment that matters.

6. *Initiate Action with Seamless Experiences across Screens*

There are two ways you can activate Quantum Multi-Screening pathways today. First keep every interaction seamless: enable your customer to move from screen to screen in ways that make sense for your marketing goal. Second, use data to personalize those experiences over time, building deeper and more valuable relationships with your customers.

7. *Measure Consumer Metrics, Not Device Metrics*

Rather than hold on to legacy measurements, *think digital*. Focus on content over media; create content that supports consumer needs at each stage in their journey; and factor in metrics that align both the consumer need with marketer objectives.

Winning in the Next Wave

Why Multi-Screen Marketing Is a Clarion Call for CxOs and Boards

Rick Chavez, Chief Solutions Officer, Microsoft Advertising

As the title suggests, this is a book about multi-screen marketing. It is chock full of relevant frameworks and techniques for practitioners. It's also an important book for senior leaders, investors, and innovators who grapple with the promise and complexities of digitization.

I'd like to frame why the book should command the attention of senior leaders. But first, I need to introduce a bit of history because the first waves of digitization (mid-90s to the present) have installed some practices that aren't particularly useful for the *next* wave. We need to free ourselves from the technology-centric thinking of the past and move toward a new people-centric framework. This book outlines how to do exactly that.

Then, I'd like to offer some takeaways for executives, innovators, and investors who are anchored in digital market evolution, and inspired by the blueprint the authors have so ably crafted.

DIGITAL MARKET EVOLUTION

For many of us, the dawn of the Internet was the beginning of the commercial Internet, circa 1995, symbolized by the arrival of Netscape and the introduction of digital content experienced directly by a person—in an office setting, or at home—via a browser on a desktop computer. It was an incredible time for many because of the rush toward new business models, new consumer business ideas in particular, and the notion that innovators had the power to change the world. The focus was on technology—harnessing it, creating it, delivering it from innovator to user. Investors also saw a new category. They began to formulate growth models for consumer Internet technology quite distinct from enterprise technology. Many of the businesses had promise, but like many technology innovations, they were too early. People were intrigued, just not ready, and the customers for Web 1.0 businesses didn't materialize to sustain the ideas that were birthed during those years.

Some businesses became anchor points for consumer attention and engagement and triggered a new category—digital publishers—that competed for the "online" attention of customers (i.e., in front of a desktop computer and a browser). These publishers had the ability to invest in digital content and services people wanted. By and large, publishers taught consumers how to engage, and organized content around people's interests, behavioral profiles (versus the needs-based approach proposed in Chapter 6), and with a desktop-only focus.

More recent, the rise of mobile devices and social engagement have begun to divvy up our collective digital attention away from traditional "online" experiences. The emerging wave of digital appliances and wearables—such as Nest, or Nike Fuel—are also compelling for the power they put in the hands of people, not to mention the outside returns they may deliver to early investors.

What's the point of all this?

The point is this: Many of us in the technology and marketing sector feel another wave of digital innovation brewing, so naturally we have to ask ourselves, "What's the next wave about, and how can I be a part of it?" As innovators, incumbents, and providers of technology, we've had 20 years of experience that pushes us toward seeing the next wave as yet another technology force unfolding . . . and that is not altogether wrong. But it doesn't feel quite right, either.

Proliferating devices, media, and content—these are a given. Channels and engagement models—social or other—will continue to evolve. Technology platforms that offload work from inside enterprises to external cloud-based services will morph and develop. Whether originating from publishers, technology innovators, or enterprises, they all point in the same direction: to people. And people—at work, at home, and on-the-go—are (1) increasingly comfortable with digital technology and (2) increasingly impatient with what digital services do not yet do.

People expect more from digital technology, but not in the feature-laden way we on the supply-side of the game often think. They expect digital tech to adapt to them and their needs, not the other way around. They expect to tell technology what to do, and have it "behave" in predictable and effective ways. They don't want to *learn* it, they just want to *use* it.

To win in the next wave, we have to invert our strategic logic and start with people's needs, then work our way backwards, rather than starting with technology and working "out." Ironically, the technology challenges we are confronted with are both numerous and fascinating—as one of my colleagues likes to say, "great brain candy" for a long time to come, because we are striving for breakthroughs in personalized experiences delivered on a massive scale, and in a way that feels natural, simple, and safe.

Perhaps Arthur C. Clarke's 3rd Law is a suitable aspiration for the next wave of digital technology: "Any sufficiently advanced technology is indistinguishable from magic."

The next wave is a huge and exciting opportunity for practitioners, as well as senior leaders. It's big enough for many innovators, large and small, and compelling for their shareholders and investors. We think it has something to do with wrapping around people and their needs, at work, at home, and on-the-go, and in ways congruent with Clarke's 3rd Law.

But it prompts a question: if the next wave starts with people and their needs and works back—what needs? And here's where this book comes to our aid.

WINNING IN THE NEXT WAVE: PEOPLE-CENTRICITY

The authors articulate a simple, but powerful premise for people-centricity: it's about the "why," not just the "what," or the "how" people behave, digitally or otherwise. This helps demystify people-centricity and gives us a lens for the next wave of digital innovation:

- People follow a decision journey that is discernible—it has *five stages* irrespective of whether the person is buying shampoo, a TV, or a car.

- They take paths from one device to another, digital and physical, that follow one of *four multi-screen patterns* (e.g., social spider-webbing).

- They are in pursuit of *nine fundamental goals* that are time-tested and universal (e.g., goal-states, first introduced in Chapter 4).

- They have grooved into digital technology along eight important dimensions—or *eight digital trends* including the Value Me trend introduced in Chapter 7.

So now, this people-centric wave starts to feel doable. We have the "secret decoder ring" or, at least, some strong guidelines for how to focus our marketing efforts. The world we are in is one where digital technology isn't separate, it's integrated. There is no more online and offline—don't make those distinctions—so we in the marketing and technology sectors have to stop delivering solutions that way. The world that people want is one where they expect to activate services toward their needs, wherever they are and in whatever mode they are in (at home, at work, on-the-go). And the more they do this—the more they have a taste of this kind of future—the more they want it.

Unfortunately, this demand goes largely unfulfilled today. This book gives numerous examples where the customer is in one place, while the marketing and technology are not contextually or otherwise relevant. There are obvious, near-term gaps to fill, even as we work on some of the trickier problems such as the "Personal Cloud" challenges referenced in Chapter 7.

The essential first step, irrespective of digital market and technology forces, is to focus on engaging experiences that work the way people do, and engage where and when people expect to be engaged. Thinking through the mind's eye of the person and her decision journey—versus the marketing funnel and "conversion"—is a key step in the right direction—toward experiences people want, and new kinds of monetization that work for brands.

There is a massive opportunity ahead in helping people complete tasks, achieve goals, and fulfill needs that matter most to them. We're at the front end of a transition—dare I say transformation—that will see companies rise and fall, based on how they rally toward people-centricity. Some, let's call them Digital Opportunists, will capture underserved opportunities focused on people, their needs, and high-value activities; while others,

Digital Laggards, will hang on to existing marketing methods, product definitions, and technology silos. We can expect to see Digital Opportunists grab more and more "share of consumer intention," and see this translate to real revenue—commerce, advertising, among other opportunities—and market value.

MOBILIZING FOR THE NEXT WAVE

I have the pleasure of working with the authors and some of the digital innovators referenced in this book. I've also had the opportunity to meet many others who are in the vanguard of innovating new products, services, and management practices. All have "stacked hands" on people-centricity and have a Digital Opportunist mind-set and ambition. Here are some of the practices we have installed that might be helpful to you, as you rally your own colleagues and organizations for the next wave:

People-centricity requires a shift in mind-set. For us, this means we anchor our efforts in the frameworks presented in this book, and embrace their prescriptive power: five stages of the consumer's decision journey, irrespective of industry; four multi-screen pathways; and eight fundamental trends. While not "answers," these are essential ingredients in shaping hypotheses that guide consumer-centric solutions, campaigns, and technologies.

People-centricity starts with experiences, not media, devices, or channels. We have institutionalized "day in the life" (DILO), end-to-end scenarios as the lens for unpacking experiences and revealing high value and often underserved opportunities to help people engage with brands. To do this, we draw on a design-led approach, where highly skilled designers drive the process, as described in Chapter 7 and the auto-buyer scenario.

Insights help us frame hypotheses; design capabilities that "take these to bright" by refining, testing, and refining them again, infusing the experiences with a blend of creativity, consumer empathy, and digital savvy.

Digital marketing innovation requires interdisciplinary skill. It never ceases to amaze and delight me how "collisions" of different disciplines can yield great outcomes. Designers can mix with "big data" wizards; engineers can engage with consumer researchers and all of the above can mix with brand stewards and P&L (business) owners. By "great" outcomes, I mean ones that are compelling but also feasible and pragmatic— interdisciplinary teams are good at framing big ideas *and* vetting them efficiently.

The best experiences are "pulled" not pushed. We've found that organizing for people-centricity requires a blend of confidence and humility; confidence in that we anchor hypotheses on data and insights and humility in that we know these must be flexible to evolve with consumer engagement. This means we have to organize to bring consumers and brands into the process early and often, and experiences are "prototyped into existence" with continual market validation. As one of our colleagues likes to say, we have to be able to "pivot or persevere," week-to-week, based on what we're learning as we expose experiences to our partners and mutual customers. This model of operating requires careful governance and stakeholder engagement, not to mention people on teams who are comfortable with this "pivot or persevere" model of work.

This book has been informed by the work of many and is a blueprint that I hope will spark the work of many others. Our mission at Microsoft is to help people—in public and private organizations, at work, at home, and on-the-go—achieve their full potential. We believe that our role is to help people do more and achieve more in this next wave. This is a mission we hope many others will embrace, across the technology sector and beyond. We hope this book will both inspire you and give you tools to realize your digital potential.

NOTES

CHAPTER 1: THE SEVEN THINGS YOU NEED TO KNOW TO REACH YOUR CUSTOMERS ACROSS TELEVISIONS, COMPUTERS, TABLETS, AND MOBILE PHONES

1. The Multi-Screen Consumer, Microsoft and Wunderman, 2010.
2. Meet the Screens, Microsoft, BBDO and Ipsos OTX, 2011.
3. Cross-Screen Engagement, Microsoft, Flamingo and Ipsos OTX, 2013.

CHAPTER 2: MEET THE PEOPLE BEHIND THE SCREENS

1. Carl Jung, *The Archetypes and the Collective Unconscious.*
2. Cross-Screen Engagement, Microsoft, Flamingo and Ipsos OTX, 2013.
3. Ibid.
4. Snooty Tea Blog.

CHAPTER 3: KNOW YOUR CUSTOMERS' DECISION JOURNEY

1. Digital Divas, Microsoft and Ogilvy, 2013.
2. The Consumer Decision Journey: Retail, Microsoft and Ipsos OTX, 2013.
3. Mobile in the Consumer Journey, Microsoft, Flamingo and Ipsos OTX, 2011.
4. The Consumer Journey: Skin Care, Microsoft and Ipsos OTX, 2012.
5. The Consumer Decision Journey: Snacks, Microsoft and Ipsos OTX, 2012.
6. Ibid.
7. Ibid.
8. Ibid.
9. Ibid.
10. Ibid.
11. Ibid.
12. The Consumer Decision Journey: Auto-Buyers, Microsoft and Ipsos OTX, 2012.
13. Ibid.

14. Ibid.
15. The Consumer Decision Journey: Financial Services, Microsoft and Ipsos OTX, 2013.
16. Ibid.
17. Ibid.
18. Ibid.
19. Ibid.
20. Ibid.

CHAPTER 4: INTRODUCING QUALITY SOCIAL

1. Digital Trends 2014, Microsoft and IPG Media Labs, 2013.
2. Ibid.
3. LineaLove.com.

CHAPTER 5: SIMPLIFY YOUR MULTI-SCREEN CONTENT STRATEGY

1. Digital Trends 2014, Microsoft, IPG Medialabs and The Future Laboratory, 2013.
2. Karen Freeman, Patrick Spenner and Anna Bird, "To Keep Your Customers, Keep it Simple," *Harvard Business Review*, May 2012. http://hbr.org/2012/05/to-keep-your-customers-keep-it-simple/ar/1
3. Dynamic Logic Market Norms, Total Sponsorships excluding MSN campaigns, 2012.
4. What Moves You, Microsoft and Ipsos OTX, 2012.
5. Digital Divas, Microsoft and Omnicom, 2013.
6. The Consumer Decision Journey: Retail, Microsoft and Ipsos OTX, 2013.
7. The Consumer Decision Journey: Auto-Buyers, Microsoft and Ipsos OTX, 2012.
8. OICA.
9. eMarketer, 2013.
10. DPTS Online Survey, April 2011.
11. 1+d/8.I.G Opinion Mining Tool.

CHAPTER 6: DRIVE EFFICIENCY BY TARGETING CONSUMER NEEDS, NOT "MILLENNIALS AND MOMS"

1. Thomas L. Friedman, *The World Is Flat* (New York: Farrar, Strauss & Giroux, 2005).
2. U.S. Census Bureau, 2011.

3. *Marriage Rate Declines and Marriage Age Rises*, Pew Research, 2011.
4. Albert Esteve, Joan Garcia-Roman, Ron Lesthaeghe, and Antonio Lopez-Gay, "The Second Demographic Transition," Features in Latin America: 2010 Update. Centre d'Estudis Demografics, Universitat Autonoma de Barcelona (March 13, 2012 version).
5. Microsoft Internal, 2013.
6. Nielsen Net Ratings, 2013.
7. Cross-Screen Engagement, Microsoft, Flamingo, and Ipsos OTX, 2013.
8. United States, U.K., Canada, Australia, and Brazil.
9. Cross-Screen Engagement, Microsoft, Flamingo, and Ipsos OTX, 2013.
10. Ibid.
11. Ibid.
12. Ibid.
13. Microsoft Internal Data.

CHAPTER 7: INITIATE ACTION WITH SEAMLESS EXPERIENCES ACROSS SCREENS

1. Cross-Screen Engagement, Microsoft, Flamingo, Ipsos OTX, 2013.
2. Digital Trends, Microsoft, IPG and The Future Laboratory, 2013.
3. Ibid.
4. Ibid.
5. Ibid.
6. Ibid.
7. The Consumer Decision Journey Financial Services, Microsoft and Ipsos OTX, 2013.
8. Ericsson, 2011, http://www.ericsson.com/news/091210_2020_mobile_world_254740099_c
9. The Consumer Decision Journey: Financial Services, Microsoft, and Ipsos OTX, 2013.

INDEX

Note: Page references in *italics* refer to figures.